W9-DCF-488

MAN AND THE COSMOS
The Vision of St Maximus the Confessor

MAN AND THE COSMOS
The Vision of St Maximus
the Confessor

by
LARS THUNBERG

with a Foreword
by
A. M. ALLCHIN

ST VLADIMIR'S SEMINARY PRESS
CRESTWOOD, NEW YORK 10707
1985

Library of Congress Cataloging in Publication Data

Thunberg, Lars, 1928-
    Man and the cosmos.

    Bibliography: p.
    Includes index.
    1. Maximus, Confessor, Saint, ca. 580-662. I. Title.
BR1720.M365T48   1985   230'.14'0924   84-22157
ISBN 0-88141-019-5

BR
1720
.M365
T48
1984

MAN AND THE COSMOS
© Copyright 1985
by
ST VLADIMIR'S SEMINARY PRESS

ALL RIGHTS RESERVED

ISBN 0-88141-019-5

PRINTED IN THE UNITED STATES OF AMERICA
BY
ATHENS PRINTING COMPANY
New York, NY 10018

Contents

Foreword

St Maximus the Confessor is without question one of the greatest Fathers of the Eastern Church. Indeed he is one of the outstanding Christian thinkers of all time. Until recently however his thought has been very little known in Western Europe and North America. Only in the last thirty or forty years has he been more widely studied, particularly in France and Germany. The publication of this present book marks something of a breakthrough for Maximian studies in the English-speaking world.

Dr. Lars Thunberg's massive study of St Maximus's doctrine of man, *Microcosm and Mediator* was published in 1965. It at once established the writer as one of the outstanding authorities in this field. Now twenty years later he gives us a general overview of St Maximus' vision of man and cosmos, and sets out for us the principle dimensions of his theology. Lars Thunberg is well known in his own country not only as a theologian and a worker for Christian unity, but also as a poet of distinction. He is one who knows about the subtlety and clarity needed for the accurate use of words.

Such qualities are very necessary for anyone who will write about St Maximus. The Confessor uses words with the greatest precision. At times his style seems highly technical, almost esoteric. This is one of the reasons why his work is often difficult of access. But this difficulty arises not from confusion but from his desire to do justice both to the unity and diversity of things, to be true to the many-faceted quality of the mystery of God which he perceives in man, in the universe, in the Scriptures and above all in God's revelation of Himself made in Jesus Christ.

Indeed the whole of St Maximus' theology can be understood as a great hymn to the unity of all things, brought about through the creative and redemptive love of God: the unity of man with God and of God with man, the unity of all creation in man when he fulfills his calling to be at once microcosm and mediator, that is, the one in whom all things created are lifted up to God from whom they came. For St Maximus this is a unity in which nothing of the infinitely rich diversification of the universe is lost; all things become their true self as all are gathered up into one single complex act of adoration.

For Maximus the center and key to the whole of this process is to be found in the person and work of Jesus Christ Himself. This is why the Chalcedonian definition of the union of God and man in the person of Christ, a union without confusion, a distinction without separation, is vital for him. This is why the monothelite controversy, the argument that Christ had only one will, that the human will was swallowed up and lost in the divine will, was something on which he could not compromise. In coming into unity with God, the creation is not annihilated. "Nothing is lost, for all in love survive." Always the elements of unity and diversity, of the specific and the universal are held together in his thinking. Everywhere as the sundered fragments of the world come together, they are transcended yet preserved in a movement of growth and longing towards the end for which in the beginning they were created.

For Maximus none of this is purely abstract or theoretical. It is the person of the incarnate Word who is at the centre of all things. The incarnation of God and the corresponding deification of man, and in man of all creation, these are the focal points not only of his thought and his prayer, but also of his daily life, personal and social. For Maximus, God is constantly becoming man in man, so that man may no less constantly become God, through the grace and gift of God. Man's participation in goodness, at every level, is a participation in God Himself, who is the source of all goodness. All man's movements to realize the end for which he was created involve him ever more deeply in participation in the divine life which comes into the world and then returns to the source from which it comes. It is in going beyond himself into God, that man becomes most truly human, "whence appears," as St Maximus puts it, "the power of this reciprocal gift which deifies man for God through the love of God, and makes God man for man through His love for man, making through this whole exchange God to become man for the deification of man, and man to become God for the hominization of God. For the Word of God who is God wills always and in all things to work the mystery of his embodiment."

As Lars Thunberg points out in this study, St Maximus was a man who lived between Christian East and West, as familiar with Rome as he was with Constantinople. He suffered in his own body the tensions already developing between those two worlds, and he died for the integrity of his vision of the bringing together of all things in Christ. He is a theologian whose work has not yet been fully appreciated, but whose theology has surprising and unexpected points of relevance for our own day. It is fitting that this book published by an Orthodox publishing house and written by a Lutheran scholar, should have a forword written by an Anglican. In the man to whom it is dedicated we have one who in his thought and in his life witnessed to the utmost to the reality of the unifying, reconciling power of the divine love. May his message be heeded by Christians of our own troubled, late twentieth century.

A. M. Allchin

CHAPTER 1

Maximus the Confessor in His Own Time: A Biographical Introduction

Maximus the Confessor is undoubtedly one of the most outstanding expositors of Christian thought in the history of the Church. As a theologian, a devout monk, and a spiritual adviser, he has a legitimate claim to be understood in his historical context. Underlining his "timeless" theological validity would do him no favor, because his historical conditions are part of his genuine creativity. He is a representative of the not-yet-divided Church, and as such he is a link between the Christian East and the Christian West. But this fact does not authorize his readers to neglect the particular historical conditions in which he lived and worked. It is precisely when we see him against the background of his own time that we recognize him as a theological genius for all time.

The obvious conclusion is that we must try to understand his ecclesiastical role (enigmatic as it may be) and his theological contribution to Christian thinking, both in context. This means, too, that we must work with his texts just as they are, and only secondarily make use of them in a wider setting. And it means that whatever we may find in his formulations and positions that is hard or difficult to understand will only increase our efforts to capture the validity of his contribution. Reading the Fathers, we can never merely copy or repristinate them; we have to live with them in constant dialogue—learning, reacting, and sharing their wisdom in our hearts.

I propose, therefore, that we not only try to grasp the sum total of Maximus's thinking, but also that we be open to his texts and let them—and his thinking in general—speak to us in our own situation, as an ecumenical situation, since he himself was, and now too remains, an ecumenical figure.

In many ways, Maximus's theology covers the whole range of classical theological topics. Since, however, there has been a certain tendency in the past to restrict his relevance to special aspects of christology, we shall try to let the dimensions of his theology illuminate as many as possible of the classical subjects of theological reflection.

Maximus's texts are not always easy to understand, even for Greeks. But this does not give us any excuse for not taking his writings seriously. In some respects his terminology is somewhat scholastic, but, being an Easterner, his intention was never scholastic in any negative sense. He wanted to be precise, and he wanted to bring light to the complexity of the issues he was dealing with.

THE HISTORICAL SETTING OF
MAXIMUS THE CONFESSOR

Emperor Justinian (482-565) and Empress Theodora had ambitions to restore the great Roman Empire to its old glory under the scepter of the Christian Caesar of Constantinople, and to reestablish the peace and unity of the Church. Their ambitions and their successes (even if not permanent) formed the image of responsible imperial policy that the emperors at the time of Maximus still tried to maintain. But during the whole lifetime of Maximus, the empire found itself threatened.

The threats of disintegration—and here we must not forget that every form of disintegration was perceived as being contrary to the ideology of the Christian Empire—were of an external as well as an internal character. In relation to the world outside, the power of Byzantium was threatened by the empire of the Persians and, in addition, by the dynasty of the Sassanids, who were inspired by the anti-Christian piety of the Zoroastrians. In 615 they advanced as far as the Asian shore of the Bosporus. In the interior, two factors radically threatened the peace of the empire. First was the almost canonical tension between the ecclesiastical center of Rome and the ecclesio-political center of Constantinople. This tension, for the first time since the victory of Christianity in the Roman Empire, was developed further, with the active aid of Maximus himself, into a conflict between Church and State, and was seen as such by the representatives of the Church, particularly in Rome. Second, there was the tension that had developed after the Council of Chalcedon in 454, the split between the Chalcedonians and the non-Chalcedonians. Some of the non-Chalcedonians were Nestorians (the followers of Nestorius) whose christology supposedly had difficulties in keeping the two sides of Christ together. They were condemned at the Council of Constantinople in 553 in an effort to reconcile the other non-Chalcedonians, i.e. the Monophysites (who taught that there was only one nature in Christ), and again later when those Monophysites found themselves nevertheless in opposition to imperial policy. Still later this hostility was fully manifested when the Moslems— who became the even more victorious successors of the Persians as Byzantium's external enemy—were in fact hailed as liberators by the Monophysites. All these events took place within the lifetime of Maximus. Syria, Mesopotamia, Palestine, Persia, Egypt, and even the whole of Northern Africa were conquered by the Moslems during the period of his theological and ecclesiastical activity.

Here it is necessary to emphasize that the coincidence of the two conflicts, in spite of the fact that they were not identical in dogma or canonical rules, reinforced tensions between Church and State. In order to reconcile the Monophysites and preserve the internal peace of the empire, the emperors, supported by the patriarchs of the imperial city, often chose doctrinal positions that had to be rejected by the Orthodox, who were at that time supported by the pope. However, that very fact happened to bring together at least some Orthodox and non-Orthodox of the East. This had been a reality to some extent already in the reign of Justinian, but the tendency became more manifest at the time of Maximus, particularly during the conflict over Monotheletism. Here, however, Maximus promoted Orthodoxy against the imperial forces supporting non-Orthodox positions. So Maximus, as a defender of Orthodoxy as he understood it in his faithfulness to Chalcedon, entered into conflict with the Imperial See. This conflict lasted till the end of his life and was supported by Rome, which also gave him spiritual support.

In the preface to his famous *Novella* 6 the Emperor Justinian had written that the emperor should support the dignity of priesthood, and that priests should pray for the emperor. However, this balance in principle was never quite successful, since the concepts of peace held by the two partners were different: that of the emperor was one of political and diplomatic harmony, and that of the Church developed, thanks to the efforts of diverse confessors, into one of doctrinal unity. Consequently, the choice of the representatives of "priesthood" more and more became a choice between a non-theological personal political position on one side, the reward of which being the benevolence of the imperial power, and the more rigorous theological position of a confessor martyr on the other. A third position—of a more "ecumenical" theology in a modern sense—had become impossible; the rigorous Orthodox theology provided the only possibility, at the time, of saving for the future a truly ecumenical attitude.

Let us here recapitulate the most important events in the time of Maximus. The emperor of his youth was Heraclius, who might, politically, be characterized as the most impressive inheritor of Justinian's policy. He enjoyed considerable success in his war against the Persians. He rescued the capital and the whole empire, and at that time he also had considerable support from the populace. The famous Holy Cross, which had been discovered by Empress Helena in the Holy Land but had been removed from Jerusalem by the Persians, was reintroduced into the Holy City by Heraclius, an act of capital symbolic importance. But from Justinian, Heraclius also inherited the idea of theological reconciliation.

Supported by his patriarch Sergius, Heraclius favored a

theological compromise between the strictly Chalcedonian position and the Monophysite. The patriarch of Alexandria at the time, Cyrus, who was of the imperial viewpoint, agreed to attempt a union with the disciples of the Monophysite Severus, through a so-called *monoenergetic* formula, in which he appealed to a formulation by Pseudo-Dionysius the Areopagite (an influential 5th century theologian of Neoplatonist tendency, whose writings appeared under the name and with the authority of the Pauline disciple Dionysius the Areopagite, known from Acts 17:34). In the formula was the *one theandric energy of Christ.*

This effort, however, was not successful, thanks to the opposition of a monk by the name of Sophronius, who had been appointed patriarch of Jerusalem (and who was a friend of Maximus). That being the situation, the patriarch Sergius agreed to pronounce a patriarchal judgment (*Psephos*) in 634, forbidding the mention of either one or two volitional principles of "operation" in Christ. Sophronius and Maximus both accepted this verdict. Sophronius, however, had to accept another situation as well: Omar the Caliph invaded Palestine and entered the capital Jerusalem. He was accompanied by the patriarch, who died shortly afterwards in 638, being spiritually exhausted.

In Constantinople the efforts to achieve theological reconciliation were now intensified. In 639, the Emperor Heraclius published a statement (an *Ecthesis*), which was, substantially, a reissue of the *Psephos* but with a clearer tendency to oppose the position which argued in favor of two wills in Christ. The conflict thus became more acute. In 641, the emperor was murdered and was succeeded by the Empress Martine, who in her very obvious efforts to favor the Monophysites relied on theological advice from Pyrrhus, the new patriarch of Constantinople. After the fall of Martine, Pyrrhus was exiled to North Africa. There, at Carthage in 645, he held his famous dispute with Maximus, where the latter succeeded in convincing him that there are after all two wills in Christ— one divine and one human—since the will is a matter of *nature* (and Christ is of two natures), and not of the *person*

(in the terms the Council of Chalcedon had used to define
the unity of person, *hypostasis,* in Christ).

The position of Rome, which had been favorable to the
Psephos, now also became more rigorous. Pyrrhus, who had
been condemned by Pope John IV, traveled to Rome after
his dispute with Maximus (who accompanied him), and
there he officially rejected *Monotheletism* (the doctrine of
one will in Christ) before Pope Theodore. But in Ravenna a
short while later he returned to Monotheletism and was then
strongly condemned by Theodore.

The policies of Constantinople, however, remained the
same during the reign of the emperor Constans, who published in 647 a *Typos,* written by the new patriarch Paul II,
which in fact promulgated the doctrine of one will. The
reaction of Rome was very vigorous; it convened a council
(the Lateran Council of 649), in which Maximus was very
active, and which he himself considered to be the sixth
Ecumenical Council. That council condemned Monotheletism
and circulated this decision around the Christian world. The
emperor could not do otherwise than arrest the pope—who
was at that time Martin I—although he did not succeed in
doing so until 653, when, for a year, Pyrrhus had already
been reintroduced at Constantinople as the patriarch. Thus,
the theological policy of the emperor, on the one side, and
the papal theology, with its ecclesiastical-political implications on the other, became separated from one another without
any possibility of reconciliation. The logical outcome would
be the double martyrdom of Pope Martin and Maximus.

THE PERSONAL BIOGRAPHY OF MAXIMUS

So far we have only dealt with the personal biography
of Maximus rather obliquely. This was done on purpose, since
it would have been false to regard his biography only as a
strictly personal one in the modern sense of the word. To a
great extent Maximus acts and appears as a representative
of his time: the only legitimate historical approach to his
destiny is through the mirror of the political and theological

conflicts of his time. On the other hand, this does not mean that he was only a victim, a passive pawn in a game of chance. It is precisely against the background of the conflicts of his time that he himself appears in history as a personality basically motivated by his theological convictions. We must therefore try to sketch in a profile of his life according to its inner consistency.

The personal life of Maximus does reflect the ecclesiastical situation of his time. For him, as for that time, there was more and more clearly a choice between political compromise and martyrdom for the true faith and confession. Yet, to regard him primarily as a dogmatician and a polemical writer who served the ecclesiastical power interests of his time would be to interpret falsely the symbolic relevance of his life. It is in his capacity as a contemplative monk and a theological visionary that he assured himself a definite and authoritative place in the Christian conscience. It is indeed characteristic of his life that his enemies in ecclesiastical and political circles accused him of political crimes rather than heresies, since his spiritual theology, his monastic status, and his integrity as a thinker were so widely recognized that any accusation of heresy would have been ineffective and would have seemed simply ridiculous.

Our sources are the diverse *Acts* about him (we find them in Migne, *Patrologia Graeca,* vol. 90). There we notice, first of all, the *Relatio motionis* (the summary of his life development), written by his disciple Anastasius in 655, which presents the history of the first action against him by the imperial court. We also find there the *Vita et certamen* (his official biography) which, however, dates from a somewhat later period, itself relying on the *Acts.* Maximus's own letters (printed in vol. 91) are of course another primary source.

Maximus was born around 580, in a family of high reputation in the imperial capital, at a time when there was a relatively high degree of harmony in the empire that covered up the tensions and conflicts which were to come. He had an occasion to engage in serious general studies. All his works prove, in fact, the quality of his studies in rhetoric and philosophy. He probably devoted himself to studies until the age of 21. He utilized his education so well that he drew the attention of the Emperor Heraclius, who invited him to become a kind of personal secretary of state. Probably in those circles he already had acquired Anastasius, who was the private secretary of the empress, as a kind of personal disciple.

He probably left the court in order to enter monastic life, even though he still maintained good relations with the court. We can deduce this from the many cordial letters to John the Chamberlain (the culminating point of this correspondence, spiritually, being the famous *Letter II* on charity). About 614 he entered the monastery of Philippicus at Chrysopolis, the Asian suburb of Constantinople. Later (perhaps in 615) he moved to the monastery of St. George at Cyzicus. We know for certain, however, that he had to leave Asia Minor on account of the Persian invasion in about 630. We find him again in Africa, i.e. at Carthage, in 632, after a voyage at sea when he probably visited not only Crete but also Cyprus.

At Carthage he entered the monastery of Euchratas as a monk. The abbot was the well-known Sophronius, who in 634 (as we have mentioned) became the patriarch of Jerusalem and the first great opponent of Monotheletism. It was in the capacity of a kind of disciple to Sophronius that Maximus entered this fight, as we have already indicated.

Certainly, it was monastic devotion and experience, far more than considerations of a political-ecclesiastical character, that turned Maximus into an outstanding theologian. Above all, he was a truth-seeking thinker of a speculative kind. During his first period of monastic life (a long period) he had access to, and assimilated, a monastic tradition of practical, ascetic, and contemplative wisdom. The influence of Evagrius, the Origenist, although Origenism had been officially condemned, was considerable in this tradition, and Maximus must have succeeded in integrating it into his own orthodoxy, while at the same time refuting Origenism as an ontological and philosophical system.

Maximus, in this process of integration, obviously used as counterpoints both the dialectical system of Pseudo-Dionysius the Areopagite (without identifying himself with it) and the spiritual theology of the Cappadocian Fathers (Gregory of

Nyssa and particularly Gregory of Nazianzus). As a matter of fact, Gregory of Nazianzus became in the process one of the most quoted authorities in his own theological work.

Many scholars have studied Maximus at just this point. Proposals have even been made that there was "an Origenist crisis" in his life, but Dom Polycarp Sherwood, the American Benedictine, has definitely shown that Maximus was able, during his first period as a monk in Asia Minor, to correct Origenism (in the first volume of his *Ambiguorum Liber*). In this respect Sherwood partly corrects the position of his famous colleague Hans Urs von Balthasar.

It may be added that more recently another Maximus scholar, Juan Miguel Garrigues, O.P., has formulated a supplementary opinion on the monastic influences on Maximus, showing how it was possible for him to take this firm stand against Origenism without making a complete rupture. Garrigues has formulated it in this way: "Origen as well as Evagrius and Gregory of Nyssa were, in our opinion, read by Maximus within a wider context of spiritual tradition. . . ."[1] As Garrigues indicates, this context was the so-called Macarian tradition.

The fight against Monotheletism turned out to be far more than a theoretical dispute about one or two wills in Christ. The consequences of the doctrine of the two natures, established by the Council of Chalcedon, was at stake. Maximus's involvement was one based on deep spiritual experience. His *dyothelite position* (i.e., his defense of the position that there must be a human as well as a divine will in Christ) was well prepared in advance. On his side, it was more his respect for the authority of the *Psephos* of Patriarch Sergius than his own deepest theological convictions that made him hesitate to enter actively into the struggle from the beginning. The doctrine of the two wills is in fact—as Garrigues has shown—first of all a logical consequence of the doctrine of the two natures, if we accept the presuppositions of its time. But for Maximus perhaps it turned out to be far more than that: it became a matter of accepting fully the humanity of Christ

[1] J. M. Garrigues, *Maxime le Confesseur. La charité—avenir divin de l'homme*, Paris 1976, p. 76.

as a prerequisite of our salvation.[2] It is precisely the active coexistence of the two natures—with their wills, according to their respective natures—which forms the mystery of salvation (the *soteriological* mystery) of, in, and through Christ. Consequently, to deny the duality of wills in Christ equals, for Maximus a misunderstanding of the very core of Christ's salvific action. If no one spoke about "one single energy," as Cyrus did, there was perhaps no need to insist explicitly upon the duality of wills, but when that happened, it became inevitable to do so. Because of that, Maximus's own terminology in the field became more and more precise, for dogmatic clarity.

As I indicated above, the martyrdom of Maximus was a tragic affair. The imperial trial of Pope Martin took place in 654. The next year Martin was exiled to Cherson, where he died in September of the same year. At that time Maximus's own trial was finalized on the basis of his alleged unwillingness to communicate with the patriarchal throne of Constantinople, so he in turn was exiled to Bizya in Thrace. However, in 656, Peter, the new patriarch of Constantinople, sent a court bishop by the name of Theodosius to Bizya in an effort of reconciliation, but Maximus did not change his position. Once more he felt obliged to refuse obedience to the will of the emperor. This happened in the monastery of St. Theodore at Perberis, also in Thrace, where he lived for six years, always active through correspondence.

In 662, Maximus was brought to Constantinople, accompanied by Anastasius the Apocrisarios and Anastasius the Monk in order to be heard by a council, which was clearly Monothelite in tendency. This council condemned him and his disciples. Their right hands and their tongues were cut off, and they were sent farther away: to Lazica on the southeast short of the Black Sea. Here Maximus died in August of the same year. His cause, however, was to be victorious within a few years' time, at the Council of Constantinople in 680-681.

[2]This is pointed out in another French dissertation: F. M. Léthel, *Théologie de l'agonie du Christ. La liberté humaine du Fils de Dieu et son importance sotériologique mises en lumière par Saint Maxime Confesseur,* Paris, 1979.

MAXIMUS AS A PERSONALITY OF HIS TIME

What kind of a personality was Maximus? As I have indicated, I will try to present a preliminary evaluation on the basis of some specific attitudes and positions taken by Maximus. The first among them, a decisive choice on his part and of capital importance for the whole rest of his life, is his decision to join a monastic community.

His Conversion to Monastic Life and his Attitude as a Monk

The ancient biographer of Maximus maintains that it was the threatening Monothelite doctrine, so utterly dangerous for the Church, that caused Maximus to leave his comfortable life as a secretary at the imperial court. But this cannot be true. This is rather a proposition put forward by a hagiographer who wanted everything to suit a pattern laid out beforehand. In fact, the biographer indicates another, far more plausible reason for the move; Maximus was simply attracted to the peaceful life of a monastery, a life of "peace." The expression he uses here is *kath'hesychian,* which means "a life in peace." This does not mean that the expression used here must be interpreted in the manner of a later time, i.e. as a "hesychastic life." All the activities of Maximus during the years after his entrance into the monastery show that he became a monk out of an authentic zeal. He was energetically involved in the traditions of ascetic and contemplative life that were then current. The Evagrian tradition became very dear to him, in spite of its Origenist tendency (which he found means to refute), and he continued to use the wisdom of its experience. In particular it became clear to him that this tradition was valuable for the practical benefit of the monks.

In line with this influence, Maximus also adapted himself to the allegorizing tradition of the Alexandrine exegesis of Holy Scripture, a tradition which was inherited by the monasteries even though the monks were in general loyal to the

Orthodox doctrines of the Church. Thus, Maximus practiced the style of "gnostic sentences," the masters of which were Evagrius, Nilus, Diadochus of Photike, Macarius, and others. In fact, he himself became one of the masters of this style, as did his own disciple Thalassius. His *Centuries on Charity, The Ascetic Life, The Gnostic Centuries,* his *Commentary on the Lord's Prayer,* his *Questions to Thalassius,* his explanations of difficult passages in Gregory of Nazianzus and in Dionysius the Areopagite in the *Ambigua,* and his *Mystagogia* are all examples of this kind of a monastic literary activity.

To our surprise, we never find in Maximus—and he probably never became an abbot of any of his monasteries—a real ideology of monastic life in the sense of a theology of the monastic state itself in relation to the Church universal. But according to I.-H. Dalmais, one of the most eminent experts on Maximus, in a contribution to the book *The Theology of the Monastic Life,* the majority of the writings of Maximus are addressed to his fellow monks. It becomes clear, at the same time, that he makes no decisive distinction between the two kinds of Christian life. To him, the experiences of monastic exercise serve as a model for the imitation of the divine life, which *all* Christians are called to fulfill. It is, obviously, the deep conviction of Maximus that the monastic tradition of asceticism, contemplation, and insight into the mystery of God exists for the benefit of the whole Church, and thus has to be realized and perfected in the wider context of the life of the Church Universal.

> [Maximus] does not hesitate to present to a layman all the requisites of the monastic life. But when he addresses himself to monks, he demonstrates how all the traditional monastic instructions regarding asceticism, the struggle against the passions, and the forms of contemplation tend to secure the full expansion of that charity, which alone is in accord with Christ and alone makes us partakers of the conditions of divine life.[3]

[3]*Théologie de la vie monastique,* Paris 1961, p. 415.

For Maximus, monastic life was never an end in itself. It serves charity, i.e. a double charity toward God and toward one's neighbor. This charity, however, has as a prerequisite an ascetic attitude, which for Maximus included a rather rigorist position concerning doctrine. For that reason, too, all the political and diplomatic compromises of the imperial court became more and more intolerable for him.

Thus, Maximus was well prepared for a life as a pilgrim and a *Confessor*. Fr. Garrigues reminds us that *xeniteia*, voluntary exile, is one of the traditional forms of oriental monasticism: the monk is a pilgrim, and a traveler on earth. In the case of Maximus, this *xeniteia* was not entirely voluntary, but when events forced him in his stationary *hesychia* to take the road, he accepted this, as Fr. Garrigues says, as "an eschatological sign of God's return."[4] This means that there existed in Maximus's life and understanding a direct line between his monastic vocation and his attitude as a *confessor* and martyr.

Here, however, we have arrived at the second test of his personality, his theological development.

His Development as a Confessor and his Insistence on the Duality of Wills in Christ the Savior

Maximus did not enter into an explicitly polemical struggle against Monotheletism before he felt he saw a manifest situation where the Christian faith was at stake. This, however, is not to say that at first he hesitated in regard to Monotheletism, as some scholars have supposed. The same holds true about his attitude to Origenism. At one time, von Balthasar spoke of an Origenist crisis in the life of Maximus, but he has been forced to change his opinion. From a theological point of view, Maximus's developmental periods are hard to distinguish. His method of counter-theology and his terminological precision developed gradually.

In his fight against Monotheletism, it seems that the full consequences of the position opposite to his own only gradu-

---

[4]Garrigues, *op. cit.,* p. 41.

ally became obvious to him. When he wrote in his *Letter II,* that ". . . equally as we have only one single nature, likewise can we only have one single mind and will with regard to God and among ourselves . . ." he could not have imagined that this statement would have been interpreted as implying a Monotheletic christological position. He speaks here only about a communion of intention between man and God, and about the unification of the wills of all men on the basis of their common nature. For him the principle (*logos*) of our common human nature indicates precisely a double relationship, expressed in the double commandment of charity. The unique will here referred to is that of human nature reuniting itself according to its *logos* in the double charity toward God and men. This is, however, not to say that this double charity is to be effected on the basis of a humanity of Christ which is in fact defective, i.e. a humanity exempt of human will. On the contrary, if a communion of wills is in fact the very goal of human nature, it becomes impossible to refuse Christ the fullness of humanity.

Consequently, it is when Maximus discovered in the fullness of its implications the danger of another position than his own—i.e., the radically Monothelite position, pretending, as it were, that the salvation and perfection of humanity consisted in a kind of absorption of what is human into that which is divine, rather than in a fulfillment of what is really human—that he became actively polemical. In that capacity he not only made certain things clear, but he also fought vehemently against the anti-Chalcedonian heresy. The person fighting was still the monk who had already, in his refutation of Origenism, made crystal clear what he meant by Christian perfection, a life which consists in the total sanctification of all the possibilities inherent in human nature. This struggle, and consequently the martyrdom which was its result, was thus the logical consequence of his monastic theology.

His Evaluation of the Bishop of Rome as a
Defender of the Doctrine of the Church

During the first legal process against him, Maximus was asked why he loved the Romans and hated the Greeks. He answered: "We have not received the commandment to hate anyone. I love the Romans since we are of the same faith, and the Greeks, because we have the same language."[5] Here Maximus clearly underlined that he shared a fellowship of faith with Rome that he did not have with "the Greeks" (of Constantinople). Certainly, this might have been simply a statement of fact, but obviously the terms "Greeks" and "Romans," as they are used here, cover a conflict of theology. When the inquisitor mentioned the "the Romans," i.e. the enemies of imperial policy, he seemed to forget that the whole empire as such ought to have been understood as "Roman," as an inheritor of ancient Rome, and as a Christian empire. Thus, in fact, he underlined the distinction between an ecclesiastical community, called "Roman," and another community (it may be political, or cultural), called "Greek." Maximus, it seems, understood immediately the symbolism of this distinction, and accepted it as fact, expressing the rupture which had taken place between Church and State. "Romans" were all those who confessed the same orthodox faith; he himself was "Greek" only because he spoke "Greek." This seemingly easy acceptance of the distinction by Maximus, however, has a deeper background, which can be made clear by a second and third quotation.

In a somewhat fragmentary letter to Peter the Illustrious (from 643 or 644), which is preserved only in a Latin version, we find some explicit expressions of a very advanced theology about the position of the Bishop of Rome. Maximus simply identified the See of Rome with the Catholic Church, and he spoke of "the very holy Church of Rome, the apostolic see, which God the Word Himself and likewise all the holy Synods, according to the holy canons and the sacred defini-

[5]*Patrologia Graeca*, 90, 128 C.

tions, have received, and which owns the power in all things and for all, over all the saints who are there for the whole inhabited earth, and likewise the power to unite and to dissolve. . . ."[6] Finally, in a letter written later in Rome, he made himself even more clear in the following manner: ". . . she [the Church of Rome] has the keys of the faith and of the orthodox confession; whoever approaches her humbly, to him is opened the real and unique piety, but she closes her mouth to any heretic who speaks against the [divine] justice."[7]

This invites us to evaluate what Maximus had to say about the primacy of the pope. As Fr. Garrigues has clearly shown (in an article in *Istina,* 1976), Maximus was convinced that Rome would never give way to the pressures of Constantinople. Once more forced to consider the possibility that in the case of Monotheletism the Romans might accept a union with the Byzantines, he answered through the paradoxical words of St. Paul, and said: "The Holy Spirit condemns . . . even the angels that would proclaim anything which is contrary to the Gospel."[8] This implies that he did not want to discuss an improbable hypothesis, but would rather declare that he was prepared to die for the truth.

This statement is a good starting point for a clarification of his own attitude. His personal experience of the doctrinal position of Rome confirmed his conviction that the promises of our Lord to Peter were applicable to the Church that preserved his relics. Thus, for him the communion of the Churches expressed itself as *"a Roman communion,"* a communion with the Bishop of Rome. One must remember that for Maximus there existed only one alternative, represented by imperial policy with its link between Church and State, and that alternative could not enjoy the same promises. Even sacramental signs were missing in the latter case.

Thus when Maximus was asked whether the Christian emperor was not also a priest, he answered: "He is not,

[6]*Patr. Gr.* 91, 144 C.
[7]*Patr. Gr.* 91, 140. The translations are based on the French of Fr. Garrigues.
[8]*Patr. Gr.* 90, 121 C; *art. cit. p.* 18.

since he is not bound to the altar. . . ." Thus, the question that concerned both empire and Church, about the truly effective unity, found its only possible solution for him in the truth he had experienced theologically and ecclesiastically. For that truth, the successor of Peter was the only manifestation endued with concrete divine promises.

On the other side it was not the canonical formalities, but the actual question of confession, that caused this attitude in Maximus. It is in the true Confession of Faith that he saw the Church as one, indeed as a unity of substance, and for this reason Maximus identified his own destiny with that of the martyr Church. The power of that unity was for him an inherent power, a power from within and not from outside, a suffering power, not a triumphant one.

His Lifestyle and his Literary Style

We have already touched on a number of details about Maximus's style of life. His monastic attitude formed an integral part of his life, and his attitude as a confessor and a martyr served to intensify his monastic "style," as we have seen already. Here his polemics, his disputation with Pyrrhus, and his manner of contesting the reproaches and accusations that were directed against him during his trial all enter in.

But his style of life was also more than that, particularly in his manner of conveying his opinions and formulating his correspondence with men in positions of political or ecclesiastical power, and in his manner of meditating upon the truths he discovered in Holy Scripture, in the tradition of the Fathers, and in the Liturgy of the Church. In all these respects he was free and yet bound (he thought freely), but he accepted the authorities that the Church had accepted.

In every circumstance he formed his own opinion through deep study. He knew Origenism from within, for example, and was able to transform that knowledge into an acceptable Christian wisdom, integrated and rectified. He understood Monotheletism deeply and spiritually, and fought against it. He penetrated the texts of Holy Scripture and exegesis before he attempted to interpret them. His opinion seems never to have been "à la mode." It was always presented as a personal, catholic opinion, and as catholic (in the sense of universally Christian) this opinion had also become his very personal one.

His manner of correspondence, through letters, was as serious as the theological ideas he usually developed in those letters. Questions about our personal salvation always occupied his thinking. His letters were always so well prepared that they could be read with profit by anyone. But this did not exclude a special pastoral note, a personal appeal.

His manner of addressing the authorities was respectful (in the style that was characteristic of the Byzantine culture of his time), but one never finds in his writings an element of superficial flattery. His exquisite politeness was well related to his serious cause, and was a part of his rigorous demand for an uncontested harmony between theory and practice. This meant that he could also be as frank as the subject demanded in expressing what he understood to be the truth.

The respect he wrought in his enemies is evident all through his life. When he was asked whether the emperor would agree to send an ambassador to Rome in order to grant a proper conciliation, he answered in a manner that was truly characteristic of him: "He will certainly do it, if he is willing to imitate God, to humiliate himself in front of Him for the sake of our salvation."[9]

This was precisely his attitude as a confessor. Polemics were for him never an end in themselves. They served the cause of salvation. And thus, he could combine his doctrinal rigidity with a certain tenderness in relations with people.

In his literary style, he was never insinuating, but was rather straightforward, even if he was in all respects a Byzantine writer. Maximus knew certainly all the rhetorical extravagances of his own educational tradition, but he did not use them simply to make an impression upon his listeners or readers. His own situation was far too serious for that sort of empty elegance. He was a deep admirer of Gregory of Nazianzus, the great *Rhetor* among the Fathers, but he did not fol-

9*Patr. Gr.* 90, 160 B.

low him in his play on synonyms, rhetorical figures, etc. He loved clarity, and for that reason he always looked for distinct formulations. His definitions and aphorisms are admirable. But he also knew the complexities of Christian theological reflection. He often constructed his sentences like Chinese boxes, which have to be opened slowly and with undisturbed attention, to reach the precious final truth he wanted to communicate to his readers.

As a kind of summary and presentation of Maximus's style, there is the *Prologue* to Maximus's *Four Centuries on Charity* (a collection of sentences written in the typical monastic style), which follows below. This is very characteristic of the kind of literature that was dear to Maximus, and which he himself wanted to promote: Christian practical wisdom in a concentrated form:

> In addition to the discussion of the *Ascetic Life* [another of Maximus's most widely read monastic treatises], I have sent this one on charity to Your Reverence, Father Elpidius, arranged in four sets of a hundred according to the number of the Gospels. While it does not perhaps come up to your expectation, still it does not fall short of my ability. Your Holiness should be aware that these are not the work of my own thought; rather, I went through the writings of the holy Fathers and selected whatever might turn the mind to my subject. I have recapitulated many things in a few lines that they may be seen at a glance, for ease in memorizing. These I send to Your Sanctity with the request that you read them with kindly forbearance and hunt only profit in them, overlooking the homeliness of the style, and pray for our limited ability that is barren of any spiritual profit.
>
> I urge you not to take what I have written as a troublesome puzzle: I have merely fulfilled a command. I say this because today we are many who get involved in words; whereas those who give or receive instruction by deeds as well are few indeed. Rather,

give your best attention to each chapter. Nor will they
all, as I think, be readily understood by everybody;
on the contrary, for a great number of them will re-
quire much scrutiny, even though they seem to be
simply expressed. Perhaps something useful for the
soul will come out of them but this will wholly come
from God's grace to him who reads with a simple mind,
with fear of God, and with charity. But for him who
takes up this or any other work whatsoever, not for
the sake of spiritual profit but of ferreting out phrases
serving to revile the author, while setting up his own
conceited self as wiser, there will never come any profit
of any sort.[10]

[10]*St Maximus the Confessor: The Ascetic Life, The Four Centuries on
Charity.* Translated and Annotated by Polycarp Sherwood, O.S.B., S.T.D.,
London 1955, p. 136 f.

CHAPTER 2

The Trinitarian Dimension of
Maximus's Theology

Maximus's theology constitutes a whole. In spite of all his movements and struggles, Maximus developed a very consistent system of theology. His theological *cosmos* could be understood in terms of the different *dimensions* that are relevant in the whole of his theological universe.

In this context the Trinitarian dimension is fundamental. His theology was not one of different entities, such as we know in Western medieval scholastic tradition. Maximus was aware of the dangers of fragmentation. His system of theology was in fact a spiritual vision of the *cosmos*, of human life within that *cosmos*, and therefore of *the economy of salvation*, the salvific interplay between the human and the divine.

But it is also quite obvious that for Maximus the doctrine of the Holy Trinity is never an isolated theme within the context of his theology. It is precisely a *dimension* in it with repercussions and consequences all over the field. This can be so, however, only on account of the presuppositions underlying the details of his Trinitarian theology. Some of these he shares with all his predecessors, some others seem to be more his own.

According to Greek thinking in general, God in His essence is immobile. Consequently, motion must be due to an intrusion into the repose of the divine life. At this point, however, rest or repose remains for Maximus characteristic of the divine life, but rest may presuppose motion. God is not immobile in the sense that He cannot move, only in the sense that whatever motion He exercises is due to His own decision. It is therefore possible to conceive of divine motion in terms of a free and creative activity. This activity is an expression of God's sovereignty, but it is also an expression of His condescension toward humankind, as already manifested in His creation and His subsequent acts of salvation.

Maximus maintains the general presupposition that God is essentially immobile, but he does not agree that this implies that motion in God is only a concession to a fall that has taken place in revolt against Him. For this reason he opposed the Origenists, who thought that God had to create the present world because of a fall within the world of pure spirits which originally He had created around Himself. Thus Maximus's understanding of creation—and of salvation—as being divine motion toward that which is created is to be understood over against a Greek negation of the possibility of movement in the Being who is perfect.

In this effort to find another basis for a positive understanding of divine motion, Maximus used the Neoplatonist tendency to interpret reality in terms of *triadic* manifestations, which he felt free to see as indications, or adumbrations, of a Divine Reality that is above human reflection and consideration. Neoplatonism understood creation as a fruit of emanation from the Godhead. Although Maximus did not accept this as a definitive clue to the Trinitarian mystery, he was able to use it as a help. The mystery remains hidden, but the Godhead becomes available to human understanding through revelation. Existence does not lack traces of God's Trinitarian being, but these traces are not given as natural revelation. Thus, Neoplatonist triadic speculations, mediated through Pseudo-Dionysius, helped Maximus both to refute Origenism and to accept motion as a category available to theology as "wisdom about God." Through Trinitarian revelation, God is qualified as the One-in-Three and as engaging Himself in a process of motion because of love, a love for His created beings, a love that is part of His own mode of being as Trinity.

When we talk about the Trinity in Maximus, we are not addressing an isolated issue. Divine life is a life in Trinitarian activity, the existential consequences of which become manifest to the eye of faith. This fact is indeed of great importance, since for Maximus the Trinity remains a mystery, opening itself only to the believer. For the believer it becomes a source of life as it is given, in total dependence on God's *philanthropia,* i.e. dependence on His own active willingness to enter into communion with those He has created in His image.

TRINITARIAN THEOLOGY IN MAXIMUS'S OWN TIME

In a masterly study of Byzantine theology, John Meyendorff quotes Theodore de Régnon on the difference between the Western and Eastern emphases in Trinitarian speculation: "Latin philosophy considers the nature in itself first and proceeds to the agent; Greek philosophy considers the agent first and passes through it to find the nature. The Latins think of personality as a mode of nature; the Greeks think of nature as the content of the person."[1] If this is correct—and we know that the differences between the two spiritual climates are of a subtle nature—we must conclude that Maximus, being indeed an Eastern Christian, is not all that clear. For him the divine Triad is a matter of "hypostatic" mode, and the content of the Person is never only identical with its "natural" constitution. Perhaps here we are in fact confronted with one of many indications of Maximus's intermediary position. He is an Eastern Christian, but with a certain inclination to accept Western distinctions. (Another example is the fact that Maximus recognizes that there is an acceptable interpretation of the *filioque,* the Western addition to the Creed of Nicaea which holds that Christ proceeds from the Father *and the Son.*)

When this is said, however, one should add that behind the Trinitarian theology of Maximus the Eastern tradition remains, and in order to clarify his own position it is important to indicate this background.

[1] J. Meyendorff, *Byzantine Theology,* Fordham 1974, p. 181.

We find it first of all in the Cappadocian Fathers, who had made the necessary distinctions. For them the unique substance of Divinity, without differences of ontological degree, is to be found in the three *hypostases* (Persons) and these three hypostases possess the same divine substance. Thus, the consubstantiality of the Persons does not affect their personal life in the sense that the latter would become illusory (the Persons are more than mere modalities of a common substance). But on the other side, the hypostatic distinctions do not affect the ontological harmony between the Persons. There is a complete unity existing in three distinct Persons.

However, the oneness of God is represented in a sovereign, specific manner by the Person of the Father, who remains the source of life for the other hypostases. For this reason, very often we find in the Cappadocians and their successors a rather close identification between the Father and Divinity. The other Persons are there because of the Father, the principle of their unity.

Yet, we find in Maximus another influence on his Trinitarian theology. It may partly coincide with that of the Cappadocians, but it contains nevertheless certain particular elements. For the Cappadocians, the hypostatic distinctions in the portrait of God in His mystery are evidently based on the successive self-revelations of God, upon what He has conceded to manifest of His own being through the history of salvation. These manifestations reflect in a way the mystery of a divine Unity, at one and the same time single and threefold. But this means that the apparent tri-theism of history is corrected by the revealed mystery of the Unity of the Three-in-One. Consequently, Trinitarian theology should essentially remain a *negative theology*, i.e. a theology that has as its essence non-knowledge.

To a Gregory of Nyssa, God in Himself is an obscure light, or rather a luminous darkness. With this concept, he expressed that other influence, which I have indicated above, and which became decisive for Maximus. It was a theological influence, nourished by Neoplatonist philosophy, but made alert in a critical attitude to that philosophy—and here the position is different from that in the West. For St. Augustine, or for a Victorinus—as Hans Urs von Balthasar has shown[2] —there is a legitimate interest in demonstrating in the created world at large, or in man, the triadic traces of the divine Trinity. For the Eastern Fathers, however, and especially for Pseudo-Dionysius the Areopagite, in spite of the triads that he discovers in the hierarchies of being, every more or less direct relation between the Trinitarian mystery and those triadic adumbrations is excluded. What God is in Himself, as Unity and Trinity, is absolutely distinct from those "traces." Even for the mystical experience proper, those representations are only an illusion in comparison with the Divine truth itself. At this point Maximus is a follower of Pseudo-Dionysius, Evagrius, and Origen.

Here Maximus quotes Pseudo-Dionysius who says that the super-essential divinity of God is not at all, even if celebrated as Monad and Triad, known to us or to anybody else as Monad and Triad, since God, who can only be celebrated by us in this way, is Himself above every name.[3]

Consequently, it is to negative theology that one must attribute Trinitarian theology proper. For Maximus this principle is always valid, but it serves a cause of a somewhat different character. In his combination of the two influences—of an explicit knowledge of a revealed mystery of a divine Unity and Trinity, and the negative experience of all true knowledge of God—Maximus tries to underline the importance of the revealing activity of God, which gives us a true possibility of entering into communion with Him *without* access to the secret of His intimate life. In this way, God's absolute Unity becomes a mysterious but triadically qualified unity, which again gives Maximus a new freedom to draw, nevertheless, some Trinitarian conclusions in regard to his speculations about man and about the world (the *cosmos*).

[2]*Kosmische Liturgie*, 2nd ed., p. 91.
[3]See von Balthasar, *op. cit.,* p. 93.

MAXIMUS'S MYSTICAL THEOLOGY OF
THE DIVINE TRINITY

Gregory of Nazianzus wrote this in his "Theological ora-
tion on the Son":[4] "That is why the Monad, in moving since
the beginning to the Dyad, stood still at the Triad" (in order
to find its rest there). This notion exercised a great influence
on Maximus. He used it as a kind of general law in his
Trinitarian theology, but also in his cosmology (even in his
refutation of Origenism). Gregory here describes a movement, divine in nature, which is not a decline or a fall (as
was the fall of the spiritual beings from the original divine
Monad in Origen), but represents, on the contrary, a kind of
perfection. God Himself is mobile. He moves toward "multiplicity," thereby perfecting, or fulfilling, His nature. Movement presupposes a distance, and marks it (a duality), but in
the case of the movement of God, it is at the same time a
movement in which He finds His rest without losing Himself,
because of the presupposed duality. He expresses through
that movement His own mode of perfection.

Of course, Gregory preserved at the same time the precise
distinction between God and His creation, but Maximus felt
free nevertheless to make a cosmological application of the
idea. For him this indicates *a divine action in creation,* which
brings the latter (through man) from the original coming to
be, in a movement that is naturally given, to the rest of
eternal bliss.

Twice Maximus commented upon this text of Gregory.
The first time is in the *Ambiguorum Liber I,* and the second
is in a letter, called his *Second Letter to Thomas* (both of
which are addressed to the abbot Thomas), where he returned
to the same problem.

If we go to the second text, we can observe that Maximus
precisely underlines the aspect of perfection. For the Platon-
ists and the older Neoplatonists, the Monad (the supreme
Unity) was the perfect primary Principle. For Maximus, on
the contrary, it was precisely in the Triad that the richness

[4]*Oratio* 29, 2.

of the Monad expressed itself. According to Origen, the
Dyad could not be perfect, since it indicated in its division a
kind of falsifying materiality. Consequently, and this is Maximus's position, the inner Trinitarian movement does not
establish an ontological distinction or a multiplicity, but marks
the perfection of a living circle, the dynamics of a divine
Being who makes Himself personal.

Maximus writes: ". . . the Monad moves in virtue of its
richness, in order that the Divinity should not be poor, reduced
as it would be, in a Jewish manner, to the limitations of one
single person." And he continues: "The Triad marks the limit
in virtue of its perfection. . . . Alone, indeed, absolutely alone
in being perfect is the noncomposed being, the nondispersed
being, who escapes at the same time both the unicity of the
person, the duality of matter, and the multiplicity of essence."[5]
This alone is God, who thus becomes perfect in leaving His
unicity without becoming dual, and who realizes His essence
in the Trinity.

However, we must add another observation, which is perhaps even more important. In the fifth chapter of his Letter
to Thomas, Maximus makes a decisive distinction in regard
to the mystery of the divine Trinity, which indicates at the
same time that the latter is truly mystical and noncomprehensi-
ble for a created being. He says that in God ". . . *the nature
of His being* and *the mode of His existence*" manifest themselves simultaneously and in combination. The Trinitarian
mystery, thus, is simply this joint manifestation, to faith, of
divine essence and existence. They are also two aspects of
life for created beings, but for men they cannot coincide
except in deification, on account of the permanent tension
between the unity of nature and the multiplicity of modes.[6]

However, there are other texts where Maximus uses this
distinction more formally and distinctly. I will refer to two
of those texts. In both cases we have a Trinitarian application
of a fundamental distinction (used in his anthropology and
his doctrine of deification as well as in his christology) between the *principle of nature* (*logos physeos*) and the mode

[5]P. Canart, "La deuxième lettre à Thomas," *Byzantion* 34, p. 432.
[6]*Ibid.*, p. 432.

of existence (*tropos hyparxeos*). Fr. Sherwood (and before him Karl Holl, among others) has studied the history of this distinction and has shown that Maximus inherited it in a preliminary form from the Cappadocians, and to some extent from Leontius of Byzantium. It was also shown that Maximus developed the distinction in a rather personal and precise way, and transformed it into an effective instrument in order to solve a number of intricate theological problems.[7] Fr. Alain Riou, O.P., has presented us with the anthropological and soteriological scheme of the same distinction.[8] Thus we know fairly well the value of the distinction for Maximus. In his Trinitarian theology, it allows him to express formally the mystery of the Monad/Triad without pretending in any way to give a rational clue to it. This mystery never consists in that distinction itself, but as we have seen, in *the manner of identity* operative beyond it.

Maximus himself only said[9] that *God is Monad according to the principle of His essence* (another way of expressing the belief that His ontological unity is not affected by the fact that He is hypostatically Three-in-One), *and that He is Triad according to His mode of existence* (which means that the three hypostases are more than just modalities, since they truly constitute the personal life of God).[10]

In the second text (which is in the second part of his *Interpretation of the Lord's Prayer*) he makes it clear that all the Persons of the Holy Trinity *exist essentially* (not only accidentally), and that the Name of the Father is the unique Son, and the Reign of the Father is the Holy Spirit. God the Father is the Father of someone who carries His Name, and He is King, ruling in the Spirit.[11] Thus God *exists* in a manner that defines at the same time His true essence. Maximus expresses this a little later in the same text (and in a somewhat subordinating way) saying that God is "a unique

[7]P. Sherwood, *The Earlier Ambigua of St. Maximus the Confessor*, Rome 1955, pp. 155-168.

[8]See A. Riou, *Le monde et l'Eglise selon Maxime le Confesseur*, Paris 1973, p. 84.

[9]*Mystagogia*, ch. 23.

[10]See here Garrigues, *op. cit.*, p. 173.

[11]Cf. Riou, *op. cit.*, p. 223.

Mind which exists essentially without any cause of His being, and who has begotten the unique Word [*Logos*], existing without a special principle of being [i.e. He is Himself His own principle of being], and is the source of the unique life, which exists essentially in an eternal manner as Holy Spirit [i.e. having in Himself His proper life]."[12]

A serious question, however, is still to be considered: In all of Maximus's formulations, are we really confronted with the mystical Trinity, or perhaps rather with the economic Trinity, i.e. the Trinity seen through the history of salvation? For when he introduces a distinction such as that between essence and existence, Maximus seems to attempt an understanding of the divine mystery, even though he does not in fact speak about revelation, which is available only through the history of salvation. We must reply that it is Maximus's conviction that we do not know in any way whatsoever without revelation whether God is Monad or Triad, and it is on the basis of only that revelation that he feels free to make the distinction. But the distinction itself covers a true mystery, the mystery of the proper manner of being divine. Because of that mystery Maximus is able to establish a combination of positive and negative theology precisely at the point of the distinction. After having established this precision, he may advance in two different directions, mutually exclusive in principle, but nevertheless related: toward the Mystery beyond words and toward a Trinitarian theology of the history of salvation (in Greek terminology, a theology of "economy").

THE "ECONOMIC" TRINITY IN MAXIMUS

First of all we must, once more, look at the link between the two forms of Trinitarian theology. I quote again from Fr. Garrigues: "God is charity. What is important for Maximus is to show that Charity (as a divine quality) within the Trinitarian life transcends hypostatically the mere 'Goodness' of divine nature, and that it is this Trinitarian 'decision' which

[12]See Riou, *op. cit.*, p. 228 f.

represents the point of departure for a scheme of Charity, in which God is personally involved, since the Son finally accomplishes it in coming into existence in human nature and is finally to die in that nature."[13] The German scholar Walther Völker underlines the same idea: "Maximus always understands the incarnation as an activity of the Trinity as a whole."[14]

The distinction between *theologia* (the Trinitarian mystery of God as He is in Himself) and *oikonomia* (the mystery of His salvific dispensation, culminating in the Incarnation) is strictly upheld by Maximus. But at the same time he relates them intimately, so that a correspondence is established. The Word incarnate remains a person of the Holy Trinity, and thus the Trinitarian formula, *"the persons, in whom is and who are the unique Divinity,"* can by him be transposed without hesitation to the christological sphere: *"the natures, of which, in which is, and which are the Christ."*[15]

Thus for Maximus the history of salvation, the "economy," is never a revelation distanced from the Trinitarian life of the Godhead. It represents the divine Trinitarian life in the destiny of creation, and this not only on account of the Fall, but for the perfection of creation through Man, a man who is always the corresponding Thou, the "iconic" partner, of God. The economic Trinity is the mystery that presents itself for imitation in human life. For Maximus it is never only a question of imitating Christ the Incarnate. We are also invited to imitate the Father, who offers the Son and Himself in Him, and thus to imitate the Trinity as a whole.

This Trinitarian aspect of the economy of salvation can be illustrated by a closer study of two different texts. The first of these is taken from Maximus's *Questions to Thalassius,* and is a part of his answer to *Question 60*. Here Maximus

[13]*Op. cit.,* p. 156.
[14]W. Völker, *Maximus Confessor als Meister des geistlichen Lebens,* Wiesbaden 1965, p. 67.
[15]See Felix Heinzer, *Gottes Sohn als Mensch. Die Struktur des Menschseins Christi bei Maximus Confessor,* Freiburg 1980, pp. 30-58; and "L'explication trinitaire de l'économie chez Maxime le Confesseur," in F. Heinzer and Chr. Schönborn, *Maximus Confessor. Actes du Symposium sur Maxime le Confesseur, Fribourg, 2-5 septembre 1980,* Fribourg 1982, p. 159 ff.

mentions three types of knowledge: rational knowledge, knowledge by notion, and knowledge through direct experience, called "perceptive" knowledge. The first two types in the end give way to the third one, which is the properly mystical knowledge of God. All this is integrated into the perspective of economy of salvation. In this context Maximus writes:

> This mystery was conceived by the Father, the Son, and the Holy Spirit before all time. By the First One through proper consent [the Father, in His intimate council, consented to bring creation in this very manner to the proper knowledge of Himself]; by the Second One through personal experience [the Son incarnates in Himself the way of salvation]; and by the Third One through cooperation. As a matter of fact, the Wisdom [*gnosis*, in the Greek text] of the Father, and of the Son, and of the Holy Spirit is one, since in them essence and power are one and the same. The Father and the Holy Spirit did not ignore the Incarnation of the Son. For the fullness of the Father is found essentially in the fullness of the Son, who accomplishes, through His Incarnation, the mystery of our salvation. He is there present, not in incarnating Himself [i.e. the Father], but in giving His consent to the Incarnation of the Son. Likewise, the fullness of the Holy Spirit is found essentially in the fullness of the Son, not in that He becomes incarnate, but by cooperating at the ineffable Incarnation of the Son.[16]

It becomes obvious in this text that for Maximus the theology of the Trinitarian mystery forms a basis for his reflections upon the divine economy. Effective revelation is due to the Son, but it is the co-activity of the Three Persons in this act that secures its absolute importance.

The second text is taken from Maximus's *Interpretation of the Lord's Prayer*. It is a passage dealing with the question

[16]*Quaest. ad Thal.* 60: *Patr. Gr.* **90, 624 BC.**

of *theologia*, i.e. the true knowledge of God, and thus parallels our first text. Maximus begins by proposing that the Word (*Logos*), through its very incarnation, teaches us *theologia*, an expression which again seems to combine the mystical and the economic perspectives. He goes on to say that the Son in Himself shows, or reveals, the other two Persons. But how?

> Since the entire Father and the entire Holy Spirit were essentially and perfectly with the entire Son, even in His incarnation, without being themselves incarnated, but the Father imagined in His benevolence, and the Spirit cooperated, the Incarnation with the Son, who Himself operated it, since the Word remained in possession of His own mind and His own life, comprehensible in its essence by the Father and the Spirit alone, while at the same time He effected, out of love for man (*philanthropia*) the hypostatic union with the flesh.[17]

We notice here once more how the Trinitarian dimension of salvation in Christ is for Maximus most intimately related to mystical theology. It is certainly only through revelation that one can understand the essential secret of the act of salvation, but revelation, in its content, is made a reality at the same time on both the "historical" and on the mystical levels.

To finish this section, we should refer to Maximus's much discussed distinction between *Providence* and *Judgment*. This distinction is closely connected with his use of Origenist terminology, and consequently is also tied to his dealing with the Origenist myth of a prehistorical fall among rational beings and a consequent second creation. For example, for a person like Evagrius, "judgment" signifies the consequences of the existence established through the second creation, while "providence" means for him the divine restitution of the original Monad of spiritual beings.

On one occasion Maximus made a triadic construction,

---

[17]*Patr. Gr.* 90, 876 CD. The text is quoted in A. Riou, *op. cit.*, p. 218, and is in its Trinitarian implications commented on by Heinzer, *art. cit.*, p. 161.

which seems to be rather Origenist in character: *Monad, Providence,* and *Judgment.*[18] One might suspect that here he wanted to establish a kind of economic Trinity, but if we compare what he says in this passage with what he says in other places, it becomes clear that he refers to christology in its proper sense, and also that if there is a Trinitarian dimension here, it partly has to do with positive, or affirmative, theology. In this case the Monad refers entirely to the mystical unity of Divine Council, while Providence refers, for example, to the hypostatic union of the natures in Christ, and Judgment to the sufferings of Christ Incarnate.

Our salvation is effected through this double reality of Christ, the first part being only ontological and the second part being "moral," i.e. one of realized intention. Even when Maximus establishes a close link between the mystical and the economic perspectives, he never allows himself to speculate about a precreational world, which would be totally different from the one we know as the world in which the Second Person of the Trinity became incarnate, with the other Persons consenting and cooperating. What God is in Himself we never know, but what he reveals of Himself never contradicts His proper being and life. And for that reason Trinitarian revelation opens a special dimension both of God and of creation, where the secret of our salvation also awaits us. It is to this latter aspect that we shall now turn.

THE TRINITY AND THE COSMOS

For Maximus, as for Pseudo-Dionysius the Areopagite and others, Trinitarian theology belongs in principle to negative (or apophatic) theology (*theologia* in the proper sense). As a matter of fact, he explicity rejects the idea of finding *traces* of the Trinity in the created world. In *Ambigua* (no. 10) he writes, while commenting on the Transfiguration:

---

[18]See *Cent. gnost* 2, 16; *Patr. Gr.* 90, 1132 B; for a commentary on the text, see also H. Urs von Balthasar, *Kosmische Liturgie. Das Weltbild Maximus' des Bekenners,* 2nd ed., Einsiedeln 1961, p. 531 ff.

The light of the face of the Lord, which for the apostles surpassed human bliss, belongs to the mystical theology according to *apophasis*. In it, the blessed and holy Divinity finds itself in essence beyond the un-utterable and unknowable and exceeds infinitely all infinity. It left absolutely no trace whatsoever to be comprehended by those who were together with it, nor did he allow any being to grasp how and in what manner it is at the same time Unity and Trinity, for it does not belong to the nature of the created order to contain the Uncreated, nor can the Infinite be em-braced by finite beings.[19]

He continues with a reference to the distinction we have mentioned above, that between Providence and Judgment: "*The cataphatic mode* [i.e. the mode of positive theology] *concerns him who decides by energy about Providence and Judgment.*" (The italics are mine.)

Certain details in this quotation are important. First of all, Maximus speaks here (in a Pseudo-Dionysian manner) about the *super-mysterious* essence: God is *more* than ineffable and unutterable. This implies that we should distinguish *three levels of theology*: the "economic" level, properly speaking, where historical revelation is to be found; the level of mystical revelation included in, or behind, historical revelation; and finally, the level of nonrevelation, which is the level of the mystery proper. Second, what is hidden is the *manner* of being Unity and Trinity at the same time, not the fact itself, since that is revealed; thus one might conceive of it in an imperfect way. Third, Maximus seems to deny a natural theology without revelation, since the same cataphatic mode refers to Providence and Judgment as well as to the specific position of Christ as Revealer.

Yet, this attitude does not exclude some kind of manifesta-tion of what is hidden in the visible, as Fr. Riou has well underlined.[20] Fr. Sherwood studied a whole series of "adum-brations" of the Trinity in creation.[21]

[19]*Patr. Gr.* 91, 1168 AB.
[20]*Op. cit.*, p. 111 ff.
[21]*Op. cit.*, p. 38.

I have already indicated one of these possible adumbrations. According to Gregory of Nazianzus, "That is why the Monad, in moving since the beginning towards the Dyad, stood still at the Triad." As we have said, this text exercised a very great influence on Maximus and helped him transform the cosmological triad of the Origenists—fixity (*stasis*), motion (*kinesis*), and becoming (*genesis*)—that was linked to their cosmology of two creations, with a fall in between, into its orthodox antithesis: *becoming-motion-fixity*.[22] For if God Himself, who is the One Who Is, moves in order to find His perfect rest (as Gregory indicates), and through this motion is not only Monad but also Triad, it is obvious that His creation is not caused by a motion that is evil in itself, but rather that there is a kind of correspondence with the Trinitarian life of God the Creator. Through this very basic fact we already have in creation a sort of "adumbration" of the Trinity, although this may never be used to expand on the mystery of God's essential life.

Let us now turn our attention to yet another capital text of Maximus, the *Questions to Thalassius*, no. 13. There Maximus seems to speak after all in terms of a kind of natural theology:

> For as by deduction from the beings we believe in regard to God who really is, *that He is,* in the same way, through their essential distinction in [different] species, we receive information regarding His essential and immanent Wisdom, that He exists and perfects the beings. Through a wise contemplation of creation we receive the idea of the holy Trinity, i.e. concerning the Father and the Son and the Holy Spirit. For the Word of God is eternal and consubstantial power and the Holy Spirit is eternal divinity.[23]

However, a closer analysis will show that we are not confronted here with a natural theology that could in any sense

---

[22]Fr. Sherwood has demonstrated this convincingly in his work *The Earlier Ambigua of St. Maximus the Confessor, and His Refutation of Origenism*, Rome 1955.

[23]*Patr. Gr.* 90, 296 B.

influence the principle of negative Trinitarian theology. For that which is said to be given to us as information through the very construction of creation is nothing else than *the naked fact* of the existence of a final Cause and of two of His qualities. Only through combining this information with that of real revelation may we arrive at a wisdom that makes us conclude that this Cause is God who is Trinity: Father, Son, and Holy Spirit. Considerations that are natural to living beings, though, do prepare us for this revelation.[24]

Another variation of the same idea is the triad *Being-Wisdom-Life,* which is, as Sherwood has shown, a modification by Maximus of an Origenist triad (Maker-Provider-Discerner) and a Pseudo-Dionysian tetrad (Goodness-Being-Life-Wisdom), going back to Neoplatonist sources. Of those two, Maximus makes an "adumbration" of the Trinity, which might serve as an image of what God is in relation to His creation. This, in turn, in some way reflects what He is in Himself, though without any indication of the *manner* in which He is Unity and Trinity at the same time.[25]

Consequently, it is not unlikely that we should also find such an adumbration in man as created in the image of God.

THE TRINITY AND THE CONSTITUTION OF MAN

Here we must start with another triad, which is strictly anthropological in character: *Being—Well-being—Ever-being.* It is related to the classical distinction in some of the earlier Fathers between image and likeness (Gn. 1:26) in the sense that "Being" and "Ever-being" refer to the image of God in man, while "Well-being" (which is included also in "Ever-being" in the blessed and perfect state of man) refers to the likeness of God in man. Now, this very distinction is not without a relationship to Trinitarian theology, for Maximus says in the first place that God communicated His proper Being to the nature of man as an image (*eikon*) of Himself, and He communicates His Goodness and His Wisdom to

---

[24]See Sherwood, *St. Maximus the Confessor: The Ascetic Life,* p. 37 ff.
[25]Sherwood, *St. Maximus the Confessor: The Ascetic Life,* p. 40

man's likeness (*homoiosis*). Then he underlines that the
secondary triads reveal, as we know, that God *is*, that He is
wise, and that He is *living* (Life). This is to say that these
qualities reveal the proper *Being, Well-being,* and *Ever-being*
of God, although in an imperfect and preliminary manner.

Thus, the anthropological triad of "Being," "Well-being,"
and "Ever-being" is another "adumbration" of God's Trinitarian life, and it stands in direct relation to the distinction
in man between divine image and divine likeness. Consequently, one could expect to find in the very constitution of
man—as an image of God, destined for likeness to Him—
another "adumbration." In fact, we do find it even though
Maximus does not develop it in detail.

In his *Ambigua,* no. 7, he states that the mind, the reason,
and the spirit of man have to be conformed to their archetypes: the Great Mind, Logos, and Spirit. And in a passage
of *Ambigua,* no. 10, he confirms that this triad of the human
soul constitutes an image of the Trinitarian Archetype, but
also that its *simplicity* and *unity* reflect the divine simplicity,
that the *goodness* expressed in the imitation of the true virtues reflects the divine goodness, and finally, that the *liberation of man from all that is divisive* reflects God's activity
of unification. It is not difficult to find in these references to
three basic human activities, references to the three Persons
of the divine Trinity. The Father is the principle of unity,
the Son is the manifestation of the goodness of God, and the
Spirit is the power of unification. (There are certain similarities here to the Trinitarian/psychological speculations of St.
Augustine, but the historical evaluation of them is very difficult to ascertain.)

There are, therefore, in Maximus clear indications of a
human *imago Trinitatis* (the image of God in man understood as an image of the Trinity), and this is related to the
constitution of man and also to his spiritual potentiality.
However, in spite of this fact, Maximus seems to be rather
cautious in elaborating this aspect, obviously because his
apophatic principles warn against it. These are only imprecise
indications in an inscrutable mystery. These indications might
serve as a kind of preparation for the true revelation of this

mystery. But, and this is important, they might also serve as a model for inner-human and inter-human relations.

We have seen that for Maximus the Trinitarian dimension is there, and is undeniable, but that it is dangerous to try to explain it or develop it beyond a certain limit. At the same time it is fundamental, and it can be applied generally to all aspects of life: to creation, to the constitution of man, and to soteriology in all its phases and perspectives.

Maximus thus speaks to us—even though from a situation that is quite different from our own in its general philosophical outlook—about a manner of "seeing" and contemplating what is above every human contemplation. It is precisely because he strictly preserves the limits of human contemplation of the divine Trinitarian mystery that he opens this dimension of life to us, through his own experience and formulations, seriously reflected upon. He invites us to share with him his Trinitarian vision of cosmic and human life. Our response can only be one of reflection upon our own experience and an answer characterized by a living dialogue with the past.

As a kind of summary, I would like to refer to a text of Maximus that is of quite a different character, and which deals with the Trinitarian mystery in a liturgical context. The text is from his commentary on the Divine Liturgy, the *Mystagogia,* and it describes the attitude of a true Christian in liturgy to the Mystery of the divine Trinity.

> The soul, from this moment, is as simple and un-
> divided as possible through doctrine, having compre-
> hended in true knowledge [*gnosis*] the defining
> principles [*logoi*] of the things sensible and indivisi-
> ble. The word now brings it towards luminous theol-
> ogy. Having passed through all things, an intelligence
> equal to that of the angels is conveyed to it, as far as
> this is possible, and the Word instructs it, with the
> same amount of Wisdom, that it could comprehend
> God, one nature in three Persons: unity in nature,
> three-foldness in persons, and Trinity in persons,
> though unity in nature; unity in trinity and trinity in
> unity, not "one and the other" or "one after the

other," or "one through the other," or again "one in
the other," or "one because of the other"; but, indeed,
the one and same in itself and through itself, beside
itself, and the same with itself. It is Unity and Trinity,
having an unconfused union in an unconfused manner,
in the same way as the indistinguishable and indivisible
distance that is there: Unity according to the principle
[*logos*] of nature, i.e. of being, and not according to
composition, or conjunction, or confusion, of whatever kind, and Trinity according to the *how* "of being
and existence," i.e. not according to distinction or
diversity or differentiation of any [ontological] kind,
since the Unity is never divided through its hypostases,
nor does it exist in order to be considered in relation
to oppositional forms of being in it. The hypostases
do not own this unity through con-junction; but it is
there, each time, in itself, in another manner. For the
Holy Trinity of the hypostases [the persons] is an unconfused unity of nature and due to its single principle [*logos*] and the Holy Unity *is* Trinity through its
hypostases and due to its own manner of being [i.e.
its hypostatical manner of being].[26]

---

[26]*Mystagogia, Patr. Gr.* 91, 700 C-701 A.

CHAPTER 3

The Soteriological Dimension

Soteriology is the doctrine of salvation. For Maximus, however, soteriology in its widest and proper sense is never conceived only as that aspect of salvation that consists in man's liberation from his sinfulness. It is the doctrine (and the mystery) of man's perfection in deification, and through man the doctrine of the fulfillment of the destiny of the whole cosmos. Yet, the starting point for any soteriology is always an actual state of deficiency. All this now leads us to some preliminary remarks.

TWO INTRODUCTORY REMARKS

The first remark concerns the soteriological dimension. Every soteriology is structured according to a general pattern. The poles of this pattern are: (a) an actual situation that demands salvation; (b) a contrary situation where the goal of salvation is achieved; and (c) an agent of salvation who is operating between the other two poles in virtue of his capacity to transform situation "a" into situation "b." In Christian tradition one can observe not only that the two poles "a" and "b" mutually influence each other (so that the definition and content of the one depends on the definition and content of the other, a fact that is only natural), but also can observe that the pole "c," the agent of salvation—who in this case is Christ the Savior (specifically the Savior we know from the Biblical portrait of Christ)—Himself exercises an influence upon the two other poles.

All this now implies that in a Christian theological universe (such as that of Maximus) we should always expect that every phenomenon, every man, and every period in his life is situated somewhere within a soteriological dimension marked by the mutual relations between the three poles. As a matter of fact, it is this field of tension that constitutes the soteriological dimension; it becomes possible to analyze the place of every phenomenon in this context evaluating its position in relation to the different soteriological poles.

This leads logically to the outline of this chapter. First of all, we shall observe Maximus's manner of describing situation "a," i.e. his analysis of the need for salvation. Second, in the same way we must observe his manner of describing situation "b," i.e. his vision of achieved salvation. Finally, we shall study his portrait of the Savior and what he has to say about the divine instruments used to fulfill salvation, the moment "c." The subject is in many ways the most central of all the dimensions in Maximus's theology.

To Maximus it is what we might call the *theandric* (i.e. the divine/human) *mystery* that is the supreme divine instrument of salvation. But we must ask *in what way* this theandric mystery is instrumental in our salvation. By the very combination of the divine and the human natures through their hypostatic union in Christ? Or through a kind of cooperation of the natural forces included in them? And in the latter case, which is the decisive motor of this cooperation in a non-monoenergetic theology like that of Maximus?

According to Fr. Garrigues (in his dissertation on the concept of charity in Maximus and in an article in *Istina,* 1974) any interpretation of Maximus from a more Oriental and Eastern Orthodox point of view, and of a supposedly more or less Neoplatonic tendency, is likely to misunderstand the true genius of the Confessor. Maximus does not conceive of man's salvation or deification exclusively in terms of a gradual participation in the divine life, a conception that one would expect in the case of a Neoplatonic writer. Maximus understands it more in terms of intentional communion, of imitation and active perfection. The effective instrument of salvation, conceived in those terms, is *a "habitual" grace* (a grace of supernatural *habitus*), understood on the basis of a rather Aristotelian philosophy.

As a matter of fact, Maximus's position at this point represents a very interesting anticipation of the theology of grace to be found in the medieval West. Charity, Garrigues says, is this *supernatural* divine gift which, in a non-ontological way, constitutes the new *habitus* of the man who is being saved. Charity is for Maximus no natural human quality, for its perfection lies in the non-natural love of enemies, and even in dying for them.

However, Fr. Garrigues has not succeeded in proving the existence of this non-natural *habitus* in Maximus. I am more inclined to believe that it is the Maximian idea of a dyophysite reciprocity between God and man that is the key to his soteriology.[1]

Let me quote a text that is very decisive at this point. We find it in the *Ambigua,* no. 10:

> They say that God and man are exemplars (*paradeigmata*) one of another; and that God makes Himself man for man's sake out of love, so far as man, enabled by God through charity, deified himself; and that man is wrapped up by God in mind to the unknowable, so far as man has manifested through virtues the God by nature invisible.[2]

Garrigues comments on this text saying that Maximus, supported by his distinction between image and likeness, pushes to an extreme point "the theandric synergism, without questioning the divine priority in the initiative of grace, which in the economy of the incarnation, has restored the divine image in man."[3] The "synergism" is certainly pushed very far in this text, but I doubt whether the reference to the

---

[1] My position seems to some extent to be confirmed by Basil Studer, OSB, in his article "Zur Soteriologie des Maximus Confessor," in Heinzer—Schönborn, *op. cit.,* pp. 239-246.

[2] *Patr. Gr.,* 91, 1113 BC, trans. by Sherwood.

[3] *Op. cit.,* p. 127.

priority of the initiative of grace in the economy of the Incarnation is sufficient as an explanation. For Maximus the point is not at all the problem of the initiative. God's initiative in the economy of salvation is never contested. It is the reciprocity between God and man that constitutes the very basis of this initiative. The text describes a double movement that expresses this reciprocity (of what we might call an onto-tropological kind) in action.

My personal interpretation of this text is that by divine (eternal) condescension there exists "from the beginning" a reciprocity of natures between God and man. For this reason we are allowed to say that man is created in the image of God. This reciprocity, however, should express itself *in action*. Therefore, we also say that man is created toward the likeness of God. Likeness manifests itself on the tropological level ("moral," if we like, though in the widest possible sense), i.e. as the manner of existence on the basis of the principle of nature. (This is the famous distinction between "principle of nature," *logos physeos*, and "manner of existence," *tropos hyparxeos*, a distinction analyzed historically and in Maximus at length by Felix Heinzer in his dissertation *Gottes Sohn als Mensch*, Freiburg 1980.)

God, too, has his "manner of existence." On the inner Trinitarian level, it expresses itself in an eternal movement from Unity through Duality to Trinity. In regard to man it expresses itself (soteriologically) on the basis of the reciprocity of the Incarnation, i.e. God moves tropologically toward man in incarnating Himself. Man in turn, who had been tropologically made passive and turned in a false direction, moves toward God, activated by the divine movement, and thus divinizing himself.

One may ask whether the question of *habitus* is ever really actualized in this system of thinking. The effective instrument of salvation is rather the activation of reciprocity on the human side, as effected by the Incarnation which liberates—through the manifestation of the divine charity—*natural* powers in man related to the likeness of God for which man is destined.

Charity is not only a divine quality, but a divine-human

destiny, based on the ontological reciprocity that God established in creating man in His image and likeness. That is to
say that charity alone is the truly *theandric quality in man,*
since it is already a theandric quality in God.

After these two preliminary remarks, we turn to the different elements of our outline, and begin by analyzing Maximus's
description of that situation which demands salvation (situation "a").

THE POSITION OF MAN WHO
REQUIRES SAVING ACTION

Here we must begin with a very central observation: The
Incarnation of the Logos, according to Maximus, is not caused
or motivated *only* by the fall and by sin, but by man's position
vis-à-vis God, by what we have called the divine-human
reciprocity. Maximus shows very clearly that the Incarnation
would have taken place even without the fall. With this
understanding Maximus places himself in line with a tradition in the ancient Church that may be traced back at least to
Irenaeus of Lyon (died c. 190). According to this tradition
man is not created perfect, so his original state is never one
of human perfection. He is called to mature and to develop
his likeness to God to the point of perfection of his nature
as image of God. Likeness is thus the realization (tropological
in Maximus, as we have seen) of all that is given as possibility because of man's nature as image of God.

But in spite of that, man's actual situation is not only
one of lack of perfection, but one of sinfulness. Maximus
describes this in several texts. We will look at two of them,
his description of man in the *Ascetic Life* and in *Letter 2.*

Liber Asceticus is given the form of a dialogue between
a novice and an old man. The first question the novice puts
concerns precisely the human conditions motivating the divine
action of salvation: "What was the purpose of the Lord's
becoming man?" The old man's answer obviously is the
only possible one: "The purpose of the Lord's becoming man
was our salvation." But precisely this answer demands a

further explanation, which opens up the whole soteriological
dimension of what is also the daily life of the monastery,
since Maximus views the monastery as a place of salvation.

Thus the old man begins to describe the situation of man
in need of salvation. He says: "Listen, man, made by God
in the beginning and placed in Paradise, transgressed the
commandment and was made subject to corruption and
death." We notice here that the simple disobedience to the
divine commandment is designated as the cause of man's
misery. In this text Maximus does not explain the nature of
this disobedience, about which sufficient knowledge is presupposed, even if a little later he becomes more precise at
two points.

But first, another detail attracts our interest: man's state
of sinfulness is not a stable one, and the fall is not only a
matter of fact given once for all, for it grows successively
worse. The old man continues: "Then, though governed from
generation to generation by the various ways of God's
Providence, yet he continued to make progress in evil." And
here he adds the two more precise statements: ". . . and was
led on, by his various fleshly passions [a kind of antithesis
to the ways of Providence] to despair of life." In other
words, man successively develops the techniques of sin and
ends in mortal despair. This is the situation that demands the
Incarnation, according to the monastic theology of the *Liber
Asceticus*.[4]

In his *Letter 2*, Maximus includes in his description of
sin not only an element of demonology but also indicates a
psychological cause of the fall of man: the destructive research of his own lust. It is his affection for himself (his
self-love, *philautía*) that is the root of evil. Its effects are
disastrous: he is cut off from God, and divisions appear in
human nature.

The active agent here, however, is the Devil, the seducer,
divider, and engineer of all the vicious methods of sin
through which man tries to find *pleasure* and avoid *pain*. Yet,
in all this, man's will cooperates with the Evil One.

Maximus establishes a kind of chronology in the consecu-

---

[4]Our quotations are from *Patr. Gr.* 90, 912A, trans. by P. Sherwood.

tive fall of man. The first fatal step is his break with God, from which stems the first of three capital evils: *ignorance.* In being isolated from the creative source of his being, man concentrates upon himself in egoistic *self-love,* which is the second in this hierarchy of evils. Finally, this egoism brings man to the third evil, *tyranny against his neighbor.* These three evils represent a perverted use of the three constitutive forces of the soul: reason (*logos*), perverted into ignorance; the concupiscible, or desire (*epithumía*), perverted into sensual self-love; and the irascible, or temper (*thumós*), perverted into hatred against one's neighbor.[5]

On the basis of these two texts, and others, we may summarize the essential elements of Maximus's speculation on evil. The cause of sin is the Devil, but in close cooperation with the free will of man—sometimes to the degree that Maximus does not even mention the Devil. Freedom belongs to human nature, to man's character as a being created in the image of God, but man uses it to his own destruction. This classical idea is linked with another conviction of a Platonic tendency: evil is a completely negative phenomenon. At this point Maximus expresses himself in a way that comes very close to Pseudo-Dionysius the Areopagite. I quote from the prologue to *Questions to Thalassius:* "Evil has not had, has not now, and will never have a proper existence of its own."[6]

Thus seduced both by the Devil and by his own intermediary position in the created cosmos of a spiritual/sensual order, man allows himself to fall into sin, preferring the pleasures of the sensible world to his communion with God, and becomes ignorant, forming in himself a kind of likeness to the animals and using his intellectual capacities in a continuing search for pleasures where his self-love (his *philautía*) always directs him toward what is supposed to satisfy his sensual lust.

This pleasure, though, can never be separated from its opposite, *pain.* Maximus develops at this point a fatal dialectic (in Greek he plays with the words *hedonè,* pleasure, and *odúne,* pain). The polarity of pleasure and pain is, as a

5See *Patr. Gr.* 91, 396 D-397 A.
6Ed. Laga-Steel, p. 29.

matter of fact, introduced by God Himself into the life of sinful man as a punitive and purgative power. According to this dialectic, man always seeks to find pleasure and avoid pain, an attempt in which he will never succeed, and which is in fact the direct cause of his despair. This constitutes man's destructive development in evil, as is characteristic of Maximus's understanding of sin. Sin is never for him a fixed state, but a movement against nature that deteriorates, in the same way as a human life lived in accordance with nature would be a good movement toward the final goal of human life, which is deification.

Let us once more return to the prologue of *Questions to Thalassius* and read part of its summary on the matter:

Thus, the immense and innumerable host of passions invades men's life. Their life becomes in this way deplorable. For the human beings honor the very cause of the destruction of their existence and pursue themselves, without knowing it, the cause of their corruption. The unity of human nature falls into a thousand pieces, and human beings, like beasts, devour their own nature. In fact, in trying to obtain pleasure and avoid pain, instigated by his self-love, man invents multiple and innumerable forms of corrupted passions. If, for example, on account of pleasure, one cultivates self-love, one awakes in oneself gluttony, pride, vanity, self-conceit, avarice, greed, tyranny, arrogance, ostentation, cruelty, fury, a sense of superiority, obstinacy, contempt for others, indignity, licentiousness, prodigality, debauchery, frivolity, vaunting, slackness, insult, offence, prolixity, chatting, obscenity, and all other vices of this kind. But if self-love is hit by pain, this gives rise to wrath, envy, hate, hostility, revenge, offence, slander, calumny, gloominess, lack of hope, discomfort, false accusation of the divine Providence, indifference, dispiritedness, despondency, pusillanimity, lamentation, melancholy, bitterness, jealousy, and all the other vices that are due to lack of pleasure. The mixture of pleasure and pain causes wickedness—this is what some call the synthesis between the opposite elements of evil—and gives rise to hypocrisy, irony, cunning, dissimulation, flattery, adulation, and the other devices belonging to this mixed craftiness.[7]

Thus in Maximus a whole hierarchy of vices manifests itself within this dialectic, either—as here in the prologue of *Quaest. ad Thal.*—in the form of a nearly unlimited multitude, or (more often) in the form of the Eastern (especially Evagrian) catalogue of *eight capital vices,* beginning with gluttony and fornication and ending with vainglory and pride. The point here is, however, that the inventive power of man, which in the first place is due to his rational constitution, engages itself successively in a false search for forms of passion, irresistibly ending up in a despair that is at the same time the dead end of evil, and thus the necessary condition for an acceptance of the saving act of God in the Incarnation.

This fact undoubtedly represents the soteriological dimension of our miserable situation. All that happens in our sinful life contains this dimension and calls for the other side, the vision of a truly good and natural life where all the capacities of man are utilized for his healthy development. There the final goal of his life appears in the vision of his deification or divinization (*theosis*) by grace, on the basis of his human constitution as created in the image of God. We now turn our attention to that vision.

THE HAPPY STATE OF MAN AS CREATED IN THE IMAGE OF GOD

Maximus shows some restraint in describing this state. We look in vain in his writings for a beautiful picture of the perfect life of Adam before the fall. He simply does not seem to have believed in it. At this point he manifests a striking contrast to John of Damascus, who otherwise in many ways followed Maximus. Once he even says in an abrupt

[7]Ed. Laga-Steel, p. 33 ff.; the reader may excuse my somewhat arbitrary choice of English synonyms in these lists.

way that Adam fell into sin at the very moment of his creation.[8] Furthermore, we have already indicated that Maximus
followed the line of Irenaeus in regarding the first man as
not yet perfect.

But this does not mean that Maximus lacks a vision of
human beatitude. He expects this beatitude to be the final
fulfillment of the incarnational scheme of "salvation," prepared for man already before his fall. We shall, therefore,
have to look for this vision (the pole "b" of the general
scheme of salvation) at three points: in his ideas about the
image and likeness of God in man; in his description of a
perfect liturgy; and in his theology of deification. Each of
these themes is very vast, so within the outline of this chapter
only fragmentary indication can be given.

The *Fifteenth Anathema* of Justinian against the Origenists attacked their cyclical idea of an identity between beginning and end. Maximus provided a more subtle refutation
of Origenism. Thus, it is only natural that he himself wants
to avoid this idea. Fr. Sherwood has observed that even
Maximus sometimes seems to think in terms of an identity
between beginning and end, but in general he does not.[9]

Personally, I am inclined to think that for Maximus it
was precisely the necessity of avoiding this danger (basically
still an identification of beginning and end) that caused him
to be cautious in describing a too perfect original state of
man. He may in principle pay tribute to the state of Adam
before the fall, but he does not—as we have seen—give the
impression that he believed it had been put into practice in
an imaginable period of human history. At this point he
rather resembles the existentialist theologians of modern
times. The tribute he pays aims more at underlining the unlimited possibilities opened before man. These may be realized
in the moment when man, restored to the implications of his

[8]See *Quaest. ad Thal.* 61; *Patr. Gr.* 90, 628 A: *hama to genésthai.*

[9]In all his studies on Maximus, and at an early stage of Maximus research, Hans Urs von Balthasar struggled with the complex relationship
between Maximus and Origenism, and the possibility of an Origenist crisis
in his life, a discussion that started through an article by M. Viller in
1930. Von Balthasar shares with Sherwood the honor of having found the
key to the problem.

image character through Christ Incarnate, makes a continual effort to live out the likeness of God, which is the goal of his life.

We must notice the way Maximus makes use of the ancient distinction between the image and likeness of God in man. In fact, some of the earlier fathers and Christian writers used it, others did not. Maximus's version comes close to that of Origen, but the two are not identical. The distinction in Origen seems to indicate a certain weakness in the constitution of created man. Only the mind (the intelligence) carries the divine image, and it is in liberating himself through asceticism from his fatal relation to the body (a relation that is due to the second act of creation only) that he regains the divine likeness (constitutive of the first creation).

Maximus is not at all so straightforward, though there are certain similarities between his own position and that of Origen. But, as I have indicated before,[10] one should also ask about the influence of Diadochus of Photike (a bishop and spiritual writer who participated in the Council of Chalcedon in 451). Diadochus developed in chapter 89 of his *Gnostic Chapters* an interpretation of the distinction which resembles that of Origen. For him the likeness is above the image. It is a supernatural character and is realized in the virtues, as is the case in Origen.

Now, the position of Maximus resembles that of Diadochus too, but they are not identical. Here I return to the difference of interpretation between Fr. Garrigues and myself, which I dwelt on above. For Garrigues, the influence of Diadochus on the theology of Maximus seems to be rather important. I am inclined to think that it should be considered, but that it was not decisive.[11]

Maximus, too, says that the image of God was given to man from the beginning and that the likeness has to be acquired through a spiritual process. In fact, the distinction

[10]L. Thunberg, *Microcosm and Mediator. The theological anthropology of Maximus the Confessor,* Lund 1965.

[11]For the influence of Diadochus on Maximus at this point, see Thunberg, *op. cit.,* p. 132 ff.; and for a general statement by Garrigues on the influence of Diadochus, see Garrigues, *op. cit.,* p. 37 f.

helps to underline that process. Maximus also states that the inhabitation and formation of Christ in the Christian may be interpreted as a development of the likeness. This development is seen as a kind of imitation of God, a manifestation of the divine virtues, as in a mirror, and in general as a moral activity of man. These are all similarities in relation to Diadochus, but they are marginal.

For what concerns Maximus most of all is the central fact that I have already indicated: *the reciprocity between God and man.* On the *ontological* level this reciprocity is one between an archetype and its image. It should become manifest on the *existential* level through a double movement: God's movement toward man in the Incarnation (or in different incarnations or embodiments) and man's movement toward God in the imitative process of deification. Likeness, for Maximus, is to be found on the existential level, as we have seen several times. Man is created with a free power of determination, which has to be used freely for his *wellbeing* for an existence of good quality that is more than an ontological *status,* not because that *status* lacks something ontologically speaking, but because—as in all beings (all substances)—it should be worked out in existence, and this existence should reflect the reciprocity between God and man, i.e. a likeness. In the sense of divinization, this likeness certainly contains a supernatural aspect, but this aspect is hardly a precondition, being rather an effect.

Now, let us turn to the second vision I have indicated: *the perfect liturgy.* The reciprocity between God and man for Maximus implies a natural capacity, and even will, to move in the direction of the other. This movement does not mingle the natures, but manifests, through existential relationship, their reciprocity. In the case of God this results in Christ the Logos, in what we might call a hypostatic theandricity, which in the last instance in the case of man permits him to move, as it were, beyond himself. This "beyond" means not only beyond the natural, but also beyond the existential. At that last point Maximus refers to mysticism proper.

On this transcendence at the frontier of nature and existence Maximus makes some comments in the first of his

Theological and Economic Centuries. The text deals with
the mystery of the last three cosmic days:

> He who in a divine way has fulfilled the sixth day
> through the works and thoughts that are appropriate
> and himself with God has completed well his work
> [here a reference to the completion of God's creative
> work in six days is implied, and to the fact that all
> He created was "good"; here it is also presupposed
> that this completion on the part of man means that
> he has exercised ascetic practices, rational contempla-
> tion of things and has even cultivated his proper
> theology], he has passed in his mind all hypostasis
> which is subject to nature and time. And he is trans-
> ported to the mystical contemplation of the ages of
> ages and in an unknowable way he makes sabbath in his
> mind, in abandoning and surpassing beings entirely.
> [As I have said, we are here beyond the natural and
> the existential.] And he who is made worthy of the
> eighth day is risen from the dead—I refer to all which
> comes after God: sensible and intelligible things,
> words, and thoughts—and he lives the happy life of
> God, who alone is called and is the Life, in the sense
> that he himself becomes God through divinization.[12]

We may ask whether this vision of the final beatitude
does not presuppose both a strictly radical distinction between
image and likeness and a whole theology of supernatural
grace. Personally, I do not think so. The mystery of the
eighth day lies even beyond the level of likeness. It rests, as
it were, in the naked reciprocity of God and man. This
mystery is also beyond any *habitus* in man. Maximus is not
preoccupied with a habitual perfection, but rather with the
mystery of reciprocity as such.

This reciprocity leaves us with a kind of "empty space,"
or void, between the Uncreated and the created order (the
latter represented in man). In that "space" man moves inten-
tionally, and in that movement he is divinized without in any

[12]*Patr. Gr.* 90, 1104 AB.

way "re-cognizing" what he experiences of communion with God. There man himself is empty; he lacks the protection of his natural capacities. There remains for him only the mystery of noncomprehension, where, however, he is rewarded by God in divinization. Yet, divinization should—as other texts show—be carried out simultaneously on the level of existence through an incarnation of divine virtues in the virtues of man.

This dialectic leads us directly to mysticism proper in Maximus. What is his genuine *doctrine of deification,* the third aspect of his vision "b" as I have indicated it? Let me follow one possible way of exposition.

In this doctrine Maximus is influenced by Pseudo-Dionysius the Areopagite and by others among his predecessors. His personal contribution consists in the way in which he combines incarnation and divinization. The doctrinal basis of the deification of man is to be found in the hypostatic (personal) unity of the two natures in Christ, the consequence of which is deification in virtue of the activated relationship between the human and the divine. This consequence does not follow automatically, though, but depends on the explicit will of God in creation that man should participate in the divine nature. It is for this reason (and not exclusively because of man's fall) that the hypostatic union between human nature and the divine Logos takes place. Yet, it is characteristic of deification/divinization according to Maximus that it is effected under the precise conditions of this hypostatic union (as it was defined by the Council of Chalcedon and later explicated); it is realized in perfect coherence but without any change or violation of the natures.

This Maximian precision permits him to state two things: There is in man no natural power that can deify him, but there exists on the other hand a reciprocal relationship between God and man that permits him to become deified to the degree in which the effects of the Incarnation are conferred on him.

Man thus does not possess a natural power to become deified, but the acts of divine liberation (for example baptism) permit him to choose as his final goal (in spite of sin) that communion with God which for him constitutes perfect beatitude.

In virtue of this, a kind of "secondary incarnation" can take place in him, an incarnation in his virtues (both ascetic and theological) which reveals in a comforting way the attributes of God *and* the reciprocity between God and man. Through this revelation man becomes ready to deliver himself to the mystical void, filled by the grace of God in the form of a divinization without representations. It is thus the experience of the existential possibilities of likeness (on the basis of the human nature as created in the image of God), but not necessarily a supernatural *habitus,* that prepares him to receive—in the ontological "void"—the final divinization as noncognitive, a nongnostic mystery, a mystery which is exclusively one of divine charity.

And this is, of course, the final goal of salvation, the pole "b," in Maximus, which, however, now invites us to the additional, and decisive, inquiry about the mystery of Christ as the effective agent of this salvation.

CHRIST THE SAVIOR AS SOTERIOLOGICAL AGENT

Christology proper in Maximus, of course, requires a chapter of its own. Yet, I have chosen here not to give a fully adequate and complete description of his christology. In the next chapter we shall return to it from the point of view of the theandric dimension. What we need for the time being are some indications concerning what we might call *the christic mechanism* of Maximus's soteriology.

Maximus's doctrine of Christ's cosmic, universal, and decisive reconciliation is not entirely clear. He presents us with different aspects as, for instance, with different interpretations of the death of the Savior. As for the human side of this act, however, much light has come out of the dissertation of F. M. Léthel on the agony of Christ and Maximus's interpretation of the Gethsemane event. As in the Eastern tradition in general, Maximus puts strong stress on the Incarnation as an effective instrument of salvation, of which—at least from one point of view—the reconciling death is only a logical consequence. Thus the different aspects are complementary; the sacrificial aspect occupies no exclusive place. The incarnation itself is the supreme act of divine grace, which manifests and carries into effect the salvific relationship between God and man. But stating this, we must always remember that incarnation has to be understood in terms of the doctrine of Chalcedon. This means that incarnation does not only imply God's becoming flesh, generally speaking, but God's becoming flesh in uniting himself hypostatically with man in Christ, true God and true man, fully united but without change or fusion. In other words, incarnation is always understood by Maximus as an aspect of reciprocity. The act of salvation understood in this way is not a one-sided act so that God, as it were, "forces" His salvation on man. Nor is it a divided act so that Christ as man reconciles God the wrathful Father, as in the predominant Western tradition, but a cooperative act, an act of reciprocity, a concerted act, and it has to be understood in this way (cf. our chapter on the Trinitarian dimension).

In this perspective, then, a number of different aspects can be developed. I will mention only three of them: the sacrificial aspect, the ascetic aspect, and the gnostic aspect. The *sacrificial aspect,* in my opinion, is expressed in a passage of the *Mystagogia,* 24. There Maximus writes:

If, as He has said [referring to 2 Co. 8:9], God is the poor one in making Himself poor in condescension for us, in accepting for Himself in compassion the sufferings of the others, and in suffering mystically out of goodness until the end of time according to the measure of suffering of everyone, even more obviously will he become God, who, imitating the divine philanthropy, cures through Himself in a divine manner the sufferings of the suffering, and who manifests in his attitude the same power as God, in the analogy of the providence of salvation.[13]

[13]*Patr. Gr.* 91, 713 B.

Maximus thus says that the Incarnation implies a poverty that suffers for others, and this suffering has the validity of a model, inviting man to imitation. The reference is not to a reconciliation in the strict sense, but to a condescension to a state of suffering for those who have become His brethren. This is exactly the aspect Maximus prefers to underline: *The condescending philanthropy invites man to the very end to an imitation that liberates him from his anti-human egoism.* This imitation is carried out in terms of nature which are, however, manifest on the human level of salvation. And that in itself marks a divine victory over the Devil, who has imprisoned man in his own egoism. By representation and as a model, this scheme is realized in Christ, and when we are incorporated into Him, we are introduced into the restored dialectic of positive reciprocity, which He represents and in which salvation takes place.

The *ascetical aspect* appears, for example, in a passage of *Liber Asceticus* (chapters 10-15), where the old monk explains to the novice how Christ defeated the Devil in manifesting His absolute obedience to the double commandment of charity.

To begin with I quote from chapters 10 and 11:

> Now then, as the devil knew that there are three things by which everything human is moved—I mean food, money, and reputation, and it is by these too that he leads men down to the depths of destruction— with these same three he tempted Him in the desert. But Our Lord, becoming victor over them, ordered the devil to get behind Him. Such then is the mark of love for God.[14]

I continue with a quotation from chapter 12, where Maximus tells the history of Christ's charity toward those who have been His enemies, and who have crucified Him:

> Blasphemed, He was long-suffering; suffering, He patiently endured; He showed them every act of love.

[14]*Patr. Gr.* 90, 920 C.

Thus against the instigator He fought back by His loving-kindness toward those egged on. . . . Thus the new Adam renewed the old. . . .[15]

Maximus adds in chapter 13:

This then was the Lord's purpose, that as man He obey the Father until death, for our sake, keeping the commandment of love; that against the devil He fight back, in being subject to attack from him by means of those whom he egged on, the Scribes and Pharisees. . . .[16]

It is thus through his ascetic obedience to the double commandment of charity that Christ overcomes the Devil, liberates men, and gives us the salvific model of His imitation.

The *gnostic aspect*, finally, can be found in the *Questions to Thalassius,* 59. Here one sees immediately that the supernatural dimension is also brought to the fore, for the proper knowledge of God, according to Maximus, is given to man by divine grace. This knowledge, though, is based in man in his asceticism leading to the impassivity (*apatheia*) of all the vices, and in his natural contemplation of the ideas or principles of all created things, of their *logoi.* This is to say that his theology proper—open to man in salvation—represents a development of contemplation in negative (apophatic) terms on the basis of positive contemplation. In this text Maximus describes what Christ does for man in this regard:

. . . in uniting Himself with every man, in a manner known by Him alone, God awakes in man the sensibility which corresponds to the degree of his preparedness to receive Him, who at the end of time will be all in all.[17]

Here we are confronted with the truly supernatural

[15]*Ibid.,* 921 AB.
[16]*Ibid.,* 921 B; all the trans. by Sherwood.
[17]*Patr. Gr.* 90, 609 C.

"knowledge" of God manifested in mystical communion. It is Christ who has opened the way to this experience, but it is the reciprocity between God and man that constitutes its ontological basis. The basis that man the sinner can provide, however, is a kind of lack of knowledge, which Maximus expresses admirably, and also in an anti-Origenist way, in the same text:

> . . . man could not know his origin which was behind him. He thus tried to know his end which lay in front of him. In this way he might learn to know through the end that beginning which he had broken with, since he did not know the end through the beginning.[18]

And later he adds:

> After the transgression [of the divine will] one can no more explain the end by the beginning, but only the beginning by the end.[19]

This is obviously a very central aspect of the soteriological dimension in Maximus. With respect to nature, beginning and end are identical, even though they are not in regard to existence and likeness. But in Christ both are presented immediately to man, and this very fact liberates him from his slavery to the Devil. For this reason, there is in man (always) also a *theandric* dimension. To this dimension we shall devote our attention in the next chapter.

[18]*Ibid.*, 613 D.
[19]*Ibid.*, 616 A.

CHAPTER 4

The Theandric Dimension

The term "theandric" needs further clarification. We have used it already but only in an indefinite sense. It was in itself a very constructive innovation in the early Church. Its presupposition is christological. "Theandric" designates the entirely unique and new relationship that is established in Jesus Christ as being both fully human and fully divine: God and man as cooperating for the benefit of the whole creation, not separated and yet not mixed, not confused and yet in full harmony. One might also say that the full implications of the term "theandric" could only become apparent after the definitions of the Council of Chalcedon, where what is *theandric* in Christ is also defined as *personal*.

Maximus is among the first Christian writers to use the term frequently and freely. Thereby he introduces a whole tradition of Eastern Christian thinking, for which the reality behind the term is of the utmost importance: life itself is marked by Christ's incarnation to such an extent that there is always a theandric dimension in it. For Maximus, however, the immediate background is to be found in Pseudo-Dionysius, whose influence upon him is at this point decisive.

In his *Letter 4*, addressed to Gaius, Pseudo-Dionysius uses the expression *"the new theandric energy"* (in the first period of the Monothelite controversy this was falsified to "one theandric energy"). In *Ambigua 5* and in the *Opuscula Theologica et Polemica 7,* Maximus gives his own interpretation of this term. Maximus states that Pseudo-Dionysius's

expression should be understood in an orthodox and Chalcedonian way, i.e. as referring to both the divine and the human
energy in Christ and not to a mixture of the two. This is also
the reason why Pseudo-Dionysius does not speak of *one,* but
of the *new* theandric energy, as Maximus underlines.[1]

This "newness" of communion between the two energies
is of central importance to Maximus. For what concerns him
is precisely the active communion of the two energies. One
might even say that the term "theandric" becomes *his pre-
ferred expression of the divine-human reciprocity in action.*
The goal of the Incarnation is precisely to make possible a
communion between energies, which alone can bring into
being the divinization that is the final goal of human life.
But not only this, for divinization is in fact also the goal of
God Himself, having created in man a model corresponding
to Himself, as we saw in the last chapter.

Thus in the chapter 5 of the *Ambigua* Maximus speaks
about "the ineffable mode of mutual adhesion,"[2] which in the
economy of salvation is based on the mystery of the hypostatic
union. Maximus dares to call this mystery "identity," a term
which can easily be misunderstood if separated from its context. Consequently, it should be translated—as von Balthasar
has suggested—in a more cautious manner, as by adding "in
mutual preservation." This "identity" implies precisely that
its unified components preserve and develop their own identity in virtue of and in relation to their communion. Therefore,
Maximus also defines this "identity" as internal "invariability"
(*aparallaxía*).

The theandric dimension is thus for Maximus an affirma-
tion of the duality of natures in reciprocal communion, and
of their communion in preserved duality. This means exactly
that this dimension is the divine-human dimension as such,
seen in a cosmic, universal, and soteriological perspective.

Let us now first of all study the constitution of man in this
context.

[1]See *Patr. Gr.* 91, 85 A and 1056 B.
[2]*Ibid.,* 1056 D-1057 A.

MAN'S MICROCOSMIC CONSTITUTION AS AN ANTICIPATORY SIGN OF GOD'S INCARNATION

Maximus regards the created constitution of man as an ontological preparation for the eschatological mystery of theandrism.

Man's task is a real mission in the world, and it presupposes a theandric scheme for its complete realization. Three factors impel Maximus to the idea of *man as microcosm*: (a) his understanding of the relation between unity and multiplicity; (b) his christological interpretation of the created cosmos; and (c) the influence of the Cappadocian Fathers, who had already made use of this idea in a Christian sense. Furthermore, at this point a decisive influence should also be seen in Nemesius of Emessa.[3]

In Nemesius the idea of man as microcosm is precisely linked to a *divine task* of unifying through himself the opposed poles of the world. It is not only through his constitution which reflects the world that man is a microcosm. It is also through an act of mediation. God has placed him in an intermediary position in order to carry out this act. The very fact that the things of the world are reflected in man presents him actually with a vocation to gather them together for his and their final goal. He should relate opposite phenomena: mortal creatures with immortal creatures, rational beings with nonrational beings, etc. In this way man should function as a world in miniature, and for this reason he was created as a reflecting image of the whole cosmos.[4]

Maximus, too, underlines the active nature of the task of mediation. *Ambigua 41* is a capital text in this regard, but there are also other texts. An important one is to be found in chapters 5 and 7 of *Mystagogia,* Maximus's interpretation of the Divine Liturgy, to which we shall return particularly in chapter 5. In chapter 6 Maximus proposes, under the authority of an unknown "old man" (who might be Sophro-

---

[3]See Thunberg, *op. cit.,* p. 144 f., and for a wider treatment of the whole complex of man as microcosm, pp. 140-152.
[4]See Nemesius, *De Natura Hominis* 1; *Patr. Gr.* 40, 529 B.

nius, his spiritual master and friend), that Scripture and the universe should be contemplated as a man. Now the idea of the universe as a man is of special interest to us. This idea he develops in chapter 7. There the universe is seen as a *makranthropos*, a man enlarged. In itself this represents an opposite perspective to that of man as microcosm, but the concepts are, of course, parallel. As the world contains visible and invisible things, likewise man consists of body and soul. And this dual constitution in both cases is reflected mutually —in the sense that the intelligible things of the world represent the soul, as the soul in man represents the intelligible things, and the sensible things of the world are the type of the body, just as the body is the type of the sensible things. As there is only one man, constituted through body and soul, linked together as a unity of the same nature, so likewise is there only one world, constituted by its different elements.

This analogy between man and the universe, however, is not only a static fact. The duality should be transformed into a unity, unthreatened by dissolution. This task of unification is attributed to man as microcosm and mediator, though this task is refused by man as a sinner, who lets himself depend on the world (especially in its sensible element) rather than mastering it. Thus, only through God's Incarnation in Christ can this task or active mediation take place. Thereby it becomes a fully theandric task. The Incarnation, which was foreseen as the perfection and fulfillment of the full task of mediation, becomes its only possible cause.

This very fact now leads us to the second aspect of the theandric dimension: the Incarnation is not only (as in Origen) a kind of secondary measure, caused by the fall, but is in fact itself the law of God's plan in regard to man and the created world. Maximus emphasizes very strongly that God wills continually to make Himself incarnate, and the fall is thus only a retarding and supplementary factor in regard to this great original and eternal plan of the Triune God.

THE TRIPLE EMBODIMENT IN THE WORLD
AS A MANIFESTATION OF THE PERMANENT
DIVINE WILL TO BECOME INCARNATE

In a very central statement Maximus says that ". . . always and in all His Word God wills to effect the mystery of His embodiment [*ensomatosis*]."[5] This is also an assurance of God's final intention in regard to creation. In this context Maximus often speaks of a threefold embodiment, almost a gradual incarnation. For this reason, Alain Riou, OP, uses the term incarnation and admirably summarizes the triple embodiment:

> The incarnation of the Logos in the *logoi* of created beings at the time of the creation of the world and of the four elements, when the Spirit of God covered the waters; the incarnation of the Logos in the *logoi* of Scripture and the four Gospels, when the Spirit inspired the "prophets"; the incarnation of the Logos in our flesh, in the man "of our kind," in the humanity that is ours, realizing the fullness of the four cardinal virtues, when the Spirit covered the Virgin with His shadow.[6]

This threefold embodiment represents an economy of salvation more fundamental than one which is motivated only by the fall of man. But what does it imply?

Contemplation of the principles (*logoi*) of creation not only belongs to the natural attitude of man toward things co-created with him, but also the mediating work of the Spirit in sanctification and divinization. The reasonable (*logikos*) element in man is capable of analytical insight into created things through their *logoi*. But this insight is at the same time a gift of grace, in the sense of a willing divine communication.

[5] *Ambigua* 7; *Patr. Gr.* 91, 1084 CD, trans. by Sherwood.
[6] A. Riou, *Le monde et l'Eglise selon Maxime le Confesseur*, Paris 1973, p. 62 f.

Maximus presupposes an analogous relationship of man to the words and meanings (*logoi*) of Scripture. Embodied in the very words of Scripture, the living Logos illuminates their deepest meaning, not only in regard to their spiritual sense, but also to their ethical teachings, i.e. in regard to the *logoi* of the divine commandments. The historical Incarnation of God in Christ, the God-Man, provides us with the key to the universal cosmos and to the economy of salvation as a whole.

Unity without annihilation is the supreme divine goal. This is well illustrated in a passage of *Ambigua* 10, where Maximus teaches that the shining vestments of the transfigured Christ symbolize the fact that when God, the Sun of Righteousness, reveals Himself to the human soul, then all the *logoi* of things intelligible and sensible in Scripture and nature appear as if they were with Him.[7] Man created in the image of God is thus, according to Maximus, a key to understanding creation, not only in order that he may understand it as it is, but also that by actively understanding it in his process of divinization he may elevate it to the supreme level of its full soteriological comprehension.

Therefore, the Incarnation in its proper and historical sense can be directly related to the constitution and meaning of the cosmos. Maximus expresses this idea well in the *Questions to Thalassius,* no. 35. There he deals with the question of what it means that Christ, in becoming man, not only became flesh but also blood, and even bones, since we are called to eat the flesh, to drink the blood, and not to break the bones. The answer reveals the following considerations.

The principles (*logoi*) of intelligible beings are contemplated (and sacramentally communicated) as the Blood of Christ, and the principles (*logoi*) of sensible beings as "His visible Flesh." But Maximus goes on to consider the things which are not communicated at all in a comprehensible way. He says: "In regard to the bones, which are principles about God and superior to every comprehension, the Logos does not give them to eat." Thus the sacramental communion has this double function: to link man to the Logos as embodied

[7]*Patr. Gr.* 91, 1128.

in creation and to mark the borderline to that absolute mystery which is the hidden life of God. Here too man is a mediator, but exclusively in terms of a negative theology. The theandric reality opens itself to him at this point only through the very void that separates, and through this separation links him to that which is the proper world of the Triune God. The inclusiveness of this interpretation is clearly shown in the adjacent sections of the same text. We quote them here at full length, demonstrating their consistency with other aspects of Maximus's theological system, referred to earlier:

We can also say that the flesh of the Logos is the true virtue; that His Blood is the infallible knowledge; and that the bones are the ineffable theology. In the same way as the blood is transformed into flesh, so is knowledge transformed through practice into virtue. Besides, the principles concerning God, which are inaccessible to any intelligence and are to be found in the nature of all beings, create in an unknown way the essences of the beings in order to bring them into existence, and are constitutive links of all knowledge and all virtue, in the same way as the bones are constitutive links of the flesh and blood.

If anyone says that the flesh and blood are the principles of judgment and providence, since they will one day be carried out as food and drink, and that the bones are the ineffable principles of divinity hidden there, he expressed an acceptable opinion.

Furthermore, the flesh of the Logos is also the perfect return and restoration of human nature to itself, obtained through virtue and knowledge; the blood is the deification that is destined to bring it by grace to ever-well-being; the bones then are this unknown power itself that keeps that nature in ever-well-being.

If somebody, finally, expresses an even more subtle idea, and says that the flesh is the voluntary modifi-

cation through the virtues, and that the blood is the
perfection in truth through death (i.e. the mortification of representations), while the bones are the
primary and inaccessible principles about God which
are found in us, then even he speaks well and remains
in an appropriate insight.[8]

The supreme Maximian idea about the five mediations
of man and of Christ as his substitute and Savior expresses
this truth in an ultimate vision, which we shall deal with in
a moment. However, we might prepare ourselves through a
short analysis of another text from the *Questions to Thalassius*
(no. 60), which deals with the mystery of the Incarnation
proper—the "Christic" mystery as Maximus calls it. This
forms the basis of all that Maximus has to say about the
theandric dimension as such. It is a fairly long text, so we
shall only point to some of its details and quote a short but
central passage.

First of all, Maximus shows clearly that he is the guardian
of a rather strict version of the doctrine of Chalcedon: the
unity of the person (the *hypostasis*) of Christ does not in
any way affect the duality of the natures. Second, Maximus
insists in this text, as in so many others, on the Trinitarian
aspect of the Incarnation. We have already commented on
this aspect of the text, but an additional remark is appropriate here: Maximus forbids the introduction of the aspect
of time into Trinitarian theology in spite of the fact that one
of the persons of the holy Trinity became incarnate in time.
And yet, on the other side, he professes a Trinitarian pre-
knowledge of what the incarnate Christ will be. Thus, he
distinguishes strictly between mystical and economic theology,
while presupposing a secret link between them (see chapter
3 above).

In one place Maximus gives a subtle indication of this
matter. He says two things: (a) that the hypostatic union is
conceived eternally (and in the Trinity), and (b) that
through this union (which is the supreme expression of the
meaning of the Incarnation, as we have seen) mobile beings

[8]Ed. Laga-Steel, p. 239 ff.

may conclude their natural movement toward God, who is by nature immobile (but we might add existentially not immobile), and in doing so imitate the existential intra-Trinitarian movement and the economic incarnational divine movement toward them. It is only logical, then, that Maximus should end his exposition in this passage with a refutation of the Origenist myth about a pre-existent Monad of rational beings.

In a very central passage of the text, Maximus again gives us a clue to his incarnational thinking:

> The Logos, God by essence, became man and messenger of the divine will. He let the most intimate ground of the goodness of the Father appear, if one may say so, and showed in Himself the goal for which created beings were created. For it is for Christ, i.e. for the Christic mystery, that all time and all that is in time has received in Christ its beginning and its end. The union between the determined and the indetermined, the finite and the infinite, the limited and the non-limited, and also between Creator and creature, between rest and movement was conceived before the times. It found its accomplishment at the end of time, giving through itself fullness to the preknowledge of God. This was so in order that the beings who are mobile by nature should find Him who is by essence absolutely immobile—when their movement toward themselves and toward each other had reached its goal—and also in order that they should gain, through experience, an active knowledge of Him, in whom they were made worthy to find their rest and have in themselves, always unchangeable, the enjoyment of this knowledge.[9]

Let us now turn our attention to Maximus's vision of the *five mediations,* partly indicated in the text just quoted. Our description of it—a fairly detailed one—will constitute the third and last subsection of this chapter.

[9] *Patr. Gr.* 90, 621 BC.

THE FIVEFOLD MEDIATION OF MAN AS
A PERFECT REALIZATION OF THE THEANDRIC
DIMENSION OF THE UNIVERSE

The most impressive rendering of this vision is to be found in a central text in the *Ambigua,* number 41. We find other versions of Maximus's grand vision in *Quaest. ad Thal.* 48 and 63, but here we shall concentrate on the text of *Amb.* 41.

For Maximus, as for Nemesius of Emesa, man the microcosm is also called to be a mediator. He should do more than simply reflect the structure of the universe. His task is to lead the multiplicity and duality of the latter to a final union; this union involves, nevertheless, not violation of the differentiated natures or species, but rather their perfection. This task presented itself to man in the beginning, but its realization was interrupted by the fall. For this reason it has to be carried out first and totally by Christ, who is God and man at the same time. In Maximus's view, the Incarnation has a double motivation: both the sin of man, which prevents him from carrying out his task, and the foreseen final phase of its realization which would have been impossible for man without the Incarnation, meditating between the created and the Uncreated. For this last reason, the Incarnation would have taken place even without sin, but, after the entrance of sin through the fall, the five mediations are all first effected by Christ and by man in Him afterwards.

What are, then, the *five distinctions,* along with which mediation takes place? If we start from the top of the hierarchy, they are: (1) between the created and the Uncreated; (2) within the world of created things between the intelligible and the sensible; (3) within the sensible world between heaven and earth; (4) on earth, between paradise and the world of men; (5) in humanity between man and woman, or the masculine and the feminine. In all these cases man is assigned a special function. He should begin with his own division, the fifth, which for Maximus stands in a certain tension in relation to God's original intention for the human race. However, it is very important to notice that none of these distinctions is evil in itself, nor are they caused directly by the fall or by sin. But when sinfulness is there, the evil powers will always use these distinctions to create sinful divisions.

The mediations thus should be carried out by man—and are already carried out by Christ, though in inverted order from that of man. Thus, we are going to call the fifth mediation, which is related to the fifth distinction, the first mediation, etc. Let us analyze them one by one starting with the mediation between the sexes.

The First Mediation: Between the Sexes

According to Maximus, sexual differentiation (that is to say that part of sexuality which is related to procreation, sexual intercourse), or at least a great part of it, was brought in by God because of the fall. Before the fall another form of procreation would have been provided for man. Consequently, the first mediation is particularly applicable to those elements of created life that are separated because of sin and are against the original intention of God. The reconciliation between man and woman thus belongs to the process of purification from sin and involves for the Christian his new freedom in Christ, conveyed to him through baptism.

Here one might ask whether on this strictly human level it is at all possible to talk about a theandric dimension. We can do so, at least in one way, since all the mediations are related and form a chain. But we can do so also for another reason: it is Christ the Savior who carries out this mediation as the first. In his case, all He does as man is always correlated actively with His divine nature.

Here we must pose two special questions: (1) How does Maximus understand the man-woman duality? And (2) how is the first mediation carried out by Jesus Christ?

At the outset, it should be remembered that Maximus's evaluation of marriage is considerably higher than that of his predecessor Gregory of Nyssa, who seems to have influenced

Maximus in this matter. Yet, his general view of sexuality as
the instrument of procreation is negative, since, as we have
seen, he regards this form of procreation as a secondary
phenomenon, a substitute in time (due to the fall) for the
persistence and immortality that God wanted to give mankind. Consequently, sexuality is necessarily linked to the fatal
dialectic between pleasure and pain that appears in man's
life as a sinner. The very manner in which man is born today
is marked by his sin. But since Maximus presupposes that
God had prepared another form of human multiplication
and fertility for man the non-sinner, this negative perspective
on sexuality does not carry the implication that the generative
force of man is altogether evil. It may be used in a positive
and spiritual way. The masculine and feminine elements are
not destined to disappear, only to be subsumed effectively
under the principle (*logos*) of the common human nature.

But what does Christ do to carry out this mediation? First
of all—and now the theandric dimension is obvious—Jesus
Christ was *born* of a woman as is every man, but he was
conceived without sensual pleasure and without destruction
of the virginity of His mother. In this way Christ broke the
slavery of death for Himself and was free to accept a death
that was not forced upon Him, a voluntary death. Secondly,
in his exegesis of Galatians 3:28, Maximus identifies the
words "man" and "woman" with anger (*thumós*) and concupiscence (*epithumía*) because the sexual relationship has
become the symbol *par excellence* of the life of passions.
When the Apostle says that in Jesus Christ there is "neither
male nor female," this means that He has conquered the
passions and subordinated the forces of man under the *logos*
of his nature—and that is exactly a true mediation between
the sexes.

Now, for the Christian this has some consequences: He
has himself to transform the passions into ordered virtues
under the common principle of all that is human, i.e. he
should engage in an imitation of Christ alone who is also
the Logos, already embodied in a preliminary way in the
logoi of created beings. Marriage is not rejected; it is instituted by God Himself. But Christ has indicated a more

noble form of relationship between man and woman, a relationship *in* their common *logos* of human nature.[10]

The Second Mediation: Between Paradise and the Inhabited World

This distinction, too, is linked to the fall, and once more a reference to the common *logos* is actualized. But here it is more the aspect of *mortification* that predominates. Paradise is never for Maximus a transcendent reality. It is earth that is divided up in this way. And consequently Christ the man is in the first place the agent of this mediation. Maximus says that Christ sanctified the inhabited world (the *oikouméne*) and entered into paradise after His death, as He had promised one of the two thieves at the crucifixion. After His resurrection, in returning to the inhabited world, He manifested the restored unity of the whole world: ". . . taking part in the life of His disciples, demonstrating that the world is one and not divided against itself, because it has kept the *logos* of its being free from the division founded on difference."[11] This He does, of course, also in hypostatic communion with Himself as the divine Logos. Thus, the theandric dimension is involved.

However, Maximus's consideration of this theme contains more than that, and when we consider the whole context, the whole theandric dimension appears much more clearly.

Two specific details should be mentioned: (a) an allegorical interpretation (coming from the tradition of Origen, Gregory of Nyssa, and others) of paradise as a *place of virtues*, and (b) an exegesis of Luke 23:43, which links the conversion of the good thief with the breakdown of the fatal dialectic between pleasure and pain—and also with the same conception of a paradise of virtues which is partially based on the same earlier tradition.

This can be explained in a very concrete way. Even in Origen the allegorical interpretation of paradise as one of

[10]See *Amb.* 41; *Patr. Gr.* 91, 1309 AB.
[11]*Patr. Gr.* 91, 1309 B.

virtues does not exclude the idea of a terrestrial paradise. In
Maximus this tendency is even more explicit. He combines
the idea of a concrete and terrestrial paradise with a specific
version of the idea of a paradise of virtues. Christ opened the
way to paradise through His death and in virtue of His human
conduct. This new situation should be made manifest by
Christians, demonstrating, in imitation of Christ—and here
I cite a formulation from the *Liber Asceticus*—"a divine way
of living." This life is certainly a human life, but lived out
in a divine manner, i.e. in the theandric dimension. For
Maximus the virtuous realization of paradise functions as an
anticipation of the future life to be lived after the resurrection. This paradise of virtues is not a substitute for the visible
paradise, but it is in moral terms a manifestation of the
coherence of the whole world through the Logos.

One of the texts where Maximus develops his exegesis
of Luke 23:43 is *Ambigua* no. 53. Here Maximus presents
the good thief as a victim of his sensuality, who nevertheless
accepts the consequences of pain and who thereby gets to
know the Christ Logos present in the *logoi* of the world and
suffering because of His incarnation. He accepts the pain of
mortification and, consequently, he enters with his own *logos*
into that earth of true knowledge which is "the paradise," i.e.
a knowledge through which he comprehends the cause of his
own suffering.[12]

In another interpretation of the same text, Maximus adds
that everyone through his own nature is a double "thief"
since he consists of soul and body, but by obeying their
respective laws he may be mysteriously crucified with the
Logos because of virtue. The law of his flesh is in conflict
with the *logos* of virtue (like an imprudent thief), but the
law of the spirit is received (like a prudent thief) with the
Logos, the Savior, through the modes (*tropoi*) of the life
of moral and ascetic practice, the *vita practica*, which prepare
us for the paradise of complete insight.[13]

Other details could be added about Maximus's treatment
of this theme, but a minor addition may suffice. For Maximus

---

[12]*Amb.* 53; *Patr. Gr.* 91, 1376 AB.
[13]*Ibid.*

all the differentiated labors that present themselves to man on earth may gain a positive meaning, even if they are caused by the fact of sin, for in developing his virtues and voluntarily accepting these labors, man follows Christ on his victorious road through death to paradise. But his possibility of a true transformation of pain and suffering is opened up to us only on account of the Incarnation.

The Third Mediation: Between Heaven and Earth

We have observed that the first two mediations have a close relation to asceticism and the *vita practica*. In the case of the third mediation, it is rather the *vita contemplativa* that is the focus.

This mediation is carried out by Christ through His ascension into heaven in His earthly body, consubstantial with ours, thereby manifesting the essential *unity of sensible nature* beyond any separation.[14] This realization also implies man's restoration to his original vocation of carrying out this kind of mediation. Man should, as much as possible, let his life resemble the virtuous perfection of *the angels*. Through the suppleness of his spirit he should surmount his bodily heaviness in a permanent and spiritual ascension toward heaven, as he desires communion with God. At this point Maximus is attached to a whole complex monastic tradition that describes the spiritual life as an "angelic life," but he also combines this tradition with his own reflections.

We should also observe that the third mediation is only an intermediary stage in the contemplative ascent of the soul. The next stage is linked to the fourth mediation.

To Maximus, contemplation represents a spiritual ascent that accompanies Christ as He returns to the Father. For this reason he says that through this contemplation Christ becomes more "thin," or becomes "subtle." The descending movement of Christ in the Incarnation thus helps man to a corresponding movement of ascent. Maximus says that for someone who looks for the *logos* of God only according to

[14]See *Amb.* 41; *Patr. Gr.* 91, 1309 BC.

the flesh, the Lord does not ascend to the Father, but for those who seek it through contemplation, He does ascend to the Father.

This ascension implies in itself a kind of spiritual assimilation to the life of the angels. In his *Commentary on the Lord's Prayer*, he uses the occasion of the third demand to underline the unity between men and angels, which consists of a common individual obedience to the divine will.[15]

Yet, contemplation is also a differentiated activity, since all things are defined through their own *logoi*, as well as by those contiguous with them.

They are circumscribed by these, but at the same time all these *logoi* participate in the cosmic Logos, who is Christ present in the *logoi* of things. This fact has an important consequence. The contemplative ascent through what is in fact a utilization in "practice" of the sensible things of the *vita practica*, an ascent through which the Logos becomes more "thin," never means in Maximus's understanding that man in some way transcends the categories of the Incarnation of the Son of God. On the contrary, Maximus refers to a spiritual communion with the *body* of Christ in the state of contemplation itself, which in principle is not different from the activity effected in the virtues of the *vita practica*.

Thus the process of the third mediation can be interpreted as a form of spiritual manducation of the body of Christ, as Maximus declares in *Ambigua* no. 48. What we are concerned with is certainly a communion of the *"eyes of Christ."* He describes this communion in the following way: he who eats of the "eyes of Christ" is the one who is capable of comprehending the visible creation in a spiritual way, and consequently is also capable of gathering up the *logoi* of things, already comprehended by the senses, as well as his own soul into one single act of glorification of God.[16]

Mediation and contemplation, therefore, coincide in this effort, but both are practiced in virtue of the Incarnation of Christ, and thus also within a theandric dimension.

[15]See *Patr. Gr.* 90, 896 A-C.
[16]See *Patr. Gr.* 91, 1364 C.

The Fourth Mediation: Between the Intelligible and the Sensible

The fourth mediation unifies the sensible and the intelligible things of God's creation in a contemplation more elevated than that of the third mediation. The differentiation to be transcended thus still concerns created things. The status of intelligible things is not essentially different from that of sensible things. Both belong to the created order, and that itself is more important than their difference. This position distinguishes Maximus from the Origenists. Yet, this differentiation, too, should be transcended in mediation.

The fourth mediation was carried out by Christ in His continued ascension through the different orders of intelligible powers and principalities, the angels—Christ still being in His whole human constitution, body and soul. Human nature is thus brought by Christ through the angelic hierarchies all the way to the Father.[17]

This fact implies that Christ has revealed in Himself the common inclination of creation as a whole toward a nondivided and nondisintegrating entity in harmony with a universal *Logos,* which is in Christ. Christ's ascending movement in returning to the Father, enclothed in His humanity, through the different orders of created beings (i.e. the third and the fourth mediation) thus corresponds to creation's inherent inclination toward its unity in the Logos. This inclination is manifested by Christ on man's behalf.

Through this very fact, however, He has also shown that there is in reality only one true *logos* of the whole creation, a common principle which unifies all, even across the fundamental dichotomy between the intelligible and the sensible, and which is at the same time hidden in the good counsel of God.

As in the beginning man is called to realize this mediation in Christ *through a likeness (in knowledge) to the angels.* This implies, according to Maximus, that there is no qualitative difference between positive knowledge and supreme/

17See *Amb.* 41; *Patr. Gr.* 91, 1309 C.

mystical ignorance. The most elevated form of the "natural contemplation" belonging to this type of mediation brings man to the limit of knowledge open to him, and to the very frontier line between revelation and negative, or apophatic, theology in the proper sense.

The Fifth Mediation: Between God and His Creation

This is the mediation that man would never have been able to effect without a divine incarnation, regardless of his being created innocent. It cannot be carried out until man, as it were, leaves the sphere of creation behind and becomes united with God beyond his own nature. It is a paradoxical mediation above all the *tropoi* and *logoi* applicable to the first four.

The fifth mediation refers to a difference that separates the whole of creation from "uncreated nature," i.e. from God as He is in Himself. Yet, this does not mean that God might become comprehensible in some way. In regard to His essence and His proper qualities, there can only be complete ignorance, for there is no unity of substance between God and His creation and, consequently, no common *logos* to be utilized in common.

The *logos* and the *tropos* of our unification with God is thus above nature. This expression of Maximus is very interesting, however, since it seems to indicate a kind of *super-logical logos* that God possesses in anticipating this supreme union. Many may understand that—by analogy—there is a kind of *logos* even for this mystery, but what this *logos* is remains absolutely incomprehensible.

Yet it is revealed to faith *that* Christ has truly effected this mediation on behalf of man exclusively in virtue of His hypostatic unity of created and uncreated nature. "On behalf of man" means here that it was effected from the point of view of the humanity of Christ, through His ascension (in its final stage) as man. For from the point of view of His divinity one must say that it was effected regardless of any temporal consideration. On the other hand the point is precisely this, that this mediation should be carried out as a supreme manifestation of the theandric reality. Christ presented Himself as man before the throne of God when He had accomplished all that God had commanded us, this self-presentation *is* the fifth mediation.[18]

Christ's ascension to the right hand of the Father is the basis of this mediation, but it cannot be manifested in any external way, as in the case of the earlier mediations.

Yet, it is full of consequence in the life of the Christian. Here Maximus is of the same opinion as Gregory of Nyssa: this can only be realized in charity.[19]

The unity between God and the creation becomes manifest by grace in love, an ecstatic charity or love that directs itself continually toward God and at the same time participates continually in the love of God, always directing itself, in *philanthropia,* toward man and creation. The mystical union is a union of love, the supreme culmination of all the virtues and the perfection of all knowledge. In the next chapter we shall deal with Maximus's conception of charity in another of its aspects: the ethical and social implications.[20]

Finally, through this mediation in Christ man should *penetrate* (through a process of circumincession, *perichoresis,* analogous to that which takes place between the natures in Christ) *entirely into God* and become all that God might be, without, however, any ontological assimilation. He should receive Him as a substitute for his own ego, being compensated by the gift of God alone, through his ascension in Christ. In this way God and man are united without confusion according to the model of the hypostatic union in Christ, as it is conceived within the theological tradition of Chalcedon.

But this then also means that for Maximus the theandric dimension never ceases to be applicable. It covers the whole of human existence and the whole of creation. Through the Incarnation the cosmos has become theandric while remain-

[18]See *Amb.* 41; *Patr. Gr.* 91, 1309 C-1312 A.

[19]On the function of charity in Maximus at this point, cf. J. M. Garrigues, *op. cit.,* p. 195 ff.

[20]Fr. Garrigues has made this role of charity in Maximus's theology the theme of his dissertation.

ing wholly a created world completely separate, ontologically, from the incomprehensible reality of God.

We can conclude this chapter with a rather long quotation from *Amb.* 41 that summarizes the work of Christ in a theandric perspective:

And finally, above all, considered in His humanity He comes to God Himself, appearing, as it is written, for us as man before the face of God the Father. He who as Logos in no way whatsoever could ever be separated from the Father, accomplishing as man, in work and in truth, through an unimpeachable obedience all that He Himself as God had pre-ordered that it should be carried out. Having completed all the counsel of God the Father for us who through our misuse had made ineffective the power which was given to us by nature for this purpose from the beginning. Thus He united, first of all, ourselves in Himself through removal of the difference between male and female, manifesting us—instead of as men and women, considered primarily from the point of view of distinction—simply, in principle and in truth, as human beings, totally conformed to Him and carrying that image of His sane and entirely intact, which can in no way be affected by any symptoms of corruption. And with us and for us He embraced the whole creation through what is in the center, the extremes as being part of Himself, and He wrapped them around Himself, insolubly united with one another: Paradise and the inhabited world, heaven and earth, the sensible and the intelligible, having Himself like us a body and sensibility and soul and intellect. . . . He recapitulated in Himself all things, showing that the whole creation is one, as if it were also a man, achieved through the coming together of all its members, according to the unique, simple, undefined and indifferent principle, stating that the whole creation can have one and the same, absolutely indistinguishable logos: that of having the "non-being" before the being.[21]

Christologically Maximus later sums up the whole passage in the following way:

> The wisdom of God the Father and His understanding is the Lord Jesus Christ, who through His wisdom keeps all the species together and through the understanding of His mind embraces all single beings subsumed under them, since He is their creator and surrounds them with His providence, bringing through Himself all that is separated unto unity, calming all dissolving war among beings, and—as the Apostle says (Col. 1:20)—uniting all in peace and friendship and unsplit harmony both in heaven and on earth.[22]

---

[21]Here, as we see, Maximus at least indicates a possible content of the *logos*, which holds all creation together: that it shares the presupposition of being created, not having the source of its being in itself. *Amb.* 41; *Patr. Gr.* 91, 1309 C-1312 B.

[22]*Ibid.*, 1313 B.

CHAPTER 5

The Natural-Social Dimension

The title of this chapter simply expresses the fact that social life and virtues are seen by Maximus in the light of the nature (*physis*) of man, the nature that is common to all men, and the principle of which (the *logos* of nature) excludes any split or separation within the individual or between different human beings. One could as well speak of an ethical-social dimension, since this is in fact the subject to be treated now. However, I prefer the reference to *physis*: the common nature of all men, ruled ontologically by its principle or idea (its *logos physeos*), is the very basis of interhuman morality in Maximus.

Again the word "dimension" is important. It is not chosen at random. For Maximus morality and sociality are not isolated in his theological cosmos. They are precisely a dimension of life as a whole. The decisive proof of this is the supremacy of charity in his system, the charity or love in which the exercise of virtues culminates, that charity which is the final goal of the contemplative life of insight and also is the consummation of the mystical life. For this reason I propose an analysis of the Maximian concept of charity or love in its relationship to vices and virtues and to the final goal of human life.[1]

We begin with an analysis of Maximus's reflections on

---

[1]The theme of this chapter is treated at greater length in L. Thunberg, *op. cit.*, pp. 244-350, and is the predominant theme in Walther Völker, *Maximus Confessor als Meister des geistlichen Lebens*, Wiesbaden 1965.

the conflict between the sinful life of man and God's dual commandment of love.

THE DUAL COMMANDMENT OF LOVE AND THE CRISIS OF THE PASSIONS IN MAN

Two remarks ought to be made at the outset. Maximus in his ascetic theology is in a number of aspects a successor to the tradition of Evagrius Ponticus. This means, for example, that he inherited the hierarchy of eight capital vices, characteristic of the Evagrian system. This is an Eastern hierarchy different from the Western one: pride is not its starting point but rather its culmination. The Evagrian-Maximian hierarchy thus consists of eight vices in the following order: *gluttony, fornication, avarice, grief, wrath, listlessness, vainglory,* and *pride.* Maximus also accepts the traditional idea of the trichotomy of the human soul, i.e. he distinguishes between the *rational,* the *irascible,* and the *concupiscible* as its constitutive elements. And he combines the hierarchy of vices with the trichotomy of the soul in such a way that every vice is more or less related to one of the three elements. We can at least be certain that gluttony and fornication belong to the concupiscible element, wrath to the irascible, and vainglory and pride to the rational element. Finally, Maximus sees the virtues as positive substitutes for the vices in a virtuous man. This means that they, too, belong more or less to their own element in the human soul, even though the hierarchy of virtues is never so strictly constructed as that of the vices.

But what is even more interesting, the hierarchy of vices is seen as a manifestation of disobedience vis-à-vis the dual commandment of love. This disobedience is called self-love (*philautía*), meaning egoism, while the life of virtues is seen as manifestation of charity.[2]

[2]A penetrating study of Maximus's psychologically and spiritually remarkable analysis of self-love and of its remedy is to be found in Irenée Hausherr, S.J., *Philautie. De la tendresse pour soi à la charité selon Saint Maxime le Confesseur,* Rome 1952.

The life of vice according to Maximus is characterized by a continual disintegration. The different forms of the abuse of the natural faculties of man condition one another mutually and together destroy the positive unity of man as a composite being. No vice can satisfy man, and therefore it brings him in each case to other vices, and all the vices, especially those of the concupiscible and rational faculties, separate man from God, who is the final and integrating goal of human life. Through the vices man is also separated from his neighbor, especially through those which emanate from his irascible faculty. There are also, of course, a number of vices that are not mentioned in the hierarchy of the eight because those eight are particularly representative expressions of the various aspects of man's sinful attitude.

This disintegration of man and of humanity is contrary not only to the aim that God has placed before man. It is contrary also to the explicit double commandment of love that expresses this aim. For Maximus the trichotomist perspective is thus naturally related to a view of egoism (*philautía*) which sees it as the mother of all the vices, since self-love is a rejection of the dual commandment and of the relationships that constitute the true unity of man. In sinning, the individual sinner establishes in himself what Maximus calls an evil *gnome,* i.e. a certain predisposition of his will and his aspirations. This has the following consequences: linked to the dialectic of pleasure and pain, *philautía* generates a multitude of passions (see chapter 3 on the soteriological dimension) differentiated among themselves according to this dialectic, and thus dividing the unity of human nature into thousands of fragments. Nature is not completely destroyed, for its *logos* remains, but the outward manifestation of its unity is destroyed.

The vices cause these divisions, not only within the individual in relation to the *logos* of his nature and to the general aim of human nature as a whole, but also between him and his neighbors, since all men participate in the same nature and are called to a unity guided by this principle and aim. In separating the individual from his brethren, they also separate him from charity, for the function of charity coincides with the divine aim set before man. Separation from charity in this context means precisely this double separation from one's own true aim and from the unity of humanity. In his *Centuries on Charity* as well as in his *Letter 2* (to John the Chamberlain, on charity) Maximus underlines again and again the danger inherent in this separation from charity, while at the same time stressing the unifying function of charity itself.

The separation, thus, is always a double one: from God with His divine goal for man but also from one's neighbor and from all mankind. The duality of this separation corresponds exactly to the duality of the commandment. Further, since the two aspects of the separation are intimately related, so also the two elements of the commandment are related. Consequently, Maximus can use this duality of the commandment as a principle of analysis in relation to the different passions and vices.

In his *Centuries on Charity* (IV:75), he says, for example, that love for God is opposed to concupiscence and that love for neighbor is opposed to anger, i.e. the passion emanating from the irascible element.[3] We find a whole number of variations of this idea in Maximus. One even gets the impression that his trichotomist analysis of the vices is not only motivated by his interest in showing the links between the vices, but also by the fact that it explains the double aspect of sin as disobedience to the double commandment of love.

This impression is verified by his analysis of *philautia* as being structured in the same way. The short article IV:37 of the same *Centuries* is very interesting in this respect. Here Maximus writes: "*Be no self-pleaser and you will not hate your brothers; be no self-lover and you will love God*."[4] Maximus uses two different terms for the two aspects of self-love: the pleasing of oneself (*autareskeia*) is the weaker form applicable to the irascible element and to egoistic conduct in relation to one's neighbor, while *philautia* proper is applicable to the concupiscible element and to man's relation to God.

We may thus conclude that for Maximus the trichotomist

---

[3] *Patr. Gr.* 90, 1065 C.
[4] *Patr. Gr.* 90, 1056 C.

analysis of the vices—and the vices of the rational element, of course, also refer to our relationship with God—is intimately linked with the commandment of love. This fact corresponds with Maximus's insistence on self-love (*philautía*) as the root of all the vices and his insistence on charity as the summit of all the virtues. Man as microcosm reflects the whole created world, visible and invisible. When he suffers himself to be led by *philautía*, his microcosmic constitution brings him to vicious destruction. *Philautía* invites all the passions to exercise their disintegrating role according to the differentiation of man's nature and of the cosmos, too, as the object of man's selfish interest. But man's microcosmic constitution also helps him to function as mediator when charity in its two aspects guides him. Charity invites all the virtues to exercise their transformation of the different faculties of man, conquering the vices and utilizing them in a good cause.

Here the correspondence between the vices and the virtues is, of course, of special interest. So let us turn our attention to this problem for a moment.

CORRESPONDENCE AND NONCORRESPONDENCE BETWEEN VICES AND VIRTUES

If one compares the theological systems of Evagrius and Maximus, one is struck by a difference that concerns precisely this question of the position of charity. To Evagrius charity represents the culmination and end of the *vita practica,* but he gives a more elevated position to advancement in knowledge (*gnosis*), i.e. to the *vita contemplativa.* For Maximus, no virtue is higher than charity. In a wider sense, charity itself implies a preference to the *gnosis* of God over all other forms of knowledge, and it leads man through his intellectual activity all the way to the final communion with God. For this reason Maximus does not establish so strict a hierarchy of virtues as Evagrius does. In the case of the virtues there exists no decisive, and fatal, dialectic as there is in the case of the vices. It is the plenitude of the virtues that counts, more than their internal relations. Maximus accepts Evagrius's experience concerning the *vita practica* and also, in a certain sense, accepts charity as its summit, but for the later virtues he is more cautious in establishing a fixed hierarchy. They do not succeed each other in the sense that one simply leaves earlier virtues behind as one progresses.[5]

Maximus also, however, establishes correspondences between vices and virtues. Some examples may be mentioned: humility and meakness correspond positively to pride and vainglory; poverty to avarice; patience to wrath; self-mastery and moderation to the vices of the concupiscible element. Yet, the antitheses are not fixed in the same way as in the case of the eight vices, and this is very different from Evagrius, who establishes rather strict correspondences. If the differences and the differentiation are of interest in the case of the vices, it is rather the richness and the multitude of the virtues, active simultaneously, that dominate the picture of virtuous life.

This does not mean, however, that Maximus neglects the distribution of the virtues to the different elements of the soul. But he distributes them both in a trichotomist and a dichotomist way. The latter is the case when he concentrates his attention on man's two passible elements (the concupiscible and the irascible), where charity, as charity toward one's neighbor, is the capital virtue of the irascible element and self-mastery the capital virtue of the concupiscible element.[6]

In all circumstances, though, Maximus shows a certain reserve against a too strict correspondence. We have already seen the reasons for this, especially in his concept of charity. However, we should add another interesting consideration. It concerns his attitude to the Evagrian conception of detachment (*apátheia*), and is also linked to his particular evaluation of charity.

Evagrius understands detachment in a way similar to that of the Stoics. It is the supreme sign of the victory of asceticism, of the *vita practica,* and he sees charity as an outcome of this situation; Evagrius's conception of charity is thus colored by his passive interpretation of the *apátheia.* He regards detachment as an equilibrium of mind in a non-

[5]See further Thunberg, *op. cit.,* p. 308 ff.
[6]See *Centuries on Charity* IV:57 and IV:72.

engaged sense, as absence of concern, nonattachment and nonhostility at the same time, rather than as a positive equilibrium, e.g. in the sense of an identical charity toward all fellow human beings. The concept of a victory over the vices predominates in Evagrius. What dominates in Maximus on the contrary is the perspective of the new life as plenitude, positive engagement, equality in love, etc.

Maximus, too, has a lot to say about detachment, but it seems as if he transformed this concept itself. And if Evagrius's understanding of detachment colored his comprehension of charity, in Maximus it is the understanding of charity that colors his understanding of detachment. One can observe this tendency in the description Maximus gives of God's detachment, which man's detachment ought to imitate:[7] God is by nature good and detached, and He manifests these two attributes in loving all men alike. The aspect of balance and equilibrium, closely connected with the concept of detachment, *apátheia,* is thus transferred to the level of equality of active attitude toward others. It is precisely the combination made here between goodness and detachment that permits this change of accent in Maximus. The result is that the concept of detachment itself receives an element of activity.

The same tendency manifests itself on the human level. Maximus establishes a close link between detachment and charity. His description of the state of detachment resembles his description of charity, or better, he links them closely. The purpose is that man should be absolutely free from all vices and show perfect charity.[8] Detachment and equal charity are thus almost identical both for men and for God. In *Centuries on Charity* II:30, Maximus writes:

> He who is perfect in love and has attained the summit of detachment knows no difference between "mine and thine," between faithful and unfaithful, between slave and freeman, or indeed between male and female. Having risen above the tyranny of the passions and looking to nature, one in all men, he considers

[7]See *Centuries on Charity* I:25; *Patr. Gr.* 90, 965 B.
[8]See *ibid.,* IV:42; *Patr. Gr.* 90, 1057 A.

all equally and is disposed equally towards all. For
in Him there is neither Greek nor Jew, neither male
nor female, neither slave nor freeman, but everything
and in all things Christ.[9]

Consequently, Maximus cannot accept the position of
Evagrius, that detachment does not demand the same degree
of charity toward every man. Maximus expresses the demand
for equal charity positively, e.g. in *Centuries on Charity* I:61
and I:10, and is motivated by the fact that God is no respecter
of persons. On the contrary, this is precisely what detachment
means, even though the activity it implies is that of charity
rather than that of detachment. We may thus conclude that
the aspect of equilibrium inherent in the concept of detachment (*apátheia*) has been transformed by Maximus into a
demand for equality and nondiscrimination in the activity of
love.[10] P. Sherwood emphasizes the same difference between
Evagrius and Maximus: "In this state of charity all are loved
equally and indeed it is but one and the same love which we
extend to God and man. This is a distinct change from the
Evagrian doctrine, for whom the most that is possible is to
be without hate or rancor towards any, to maintain the calm
of detachment in their regard."[11]

But let us return once more to the divine level. We have
noticed that Maximus states that God is both good and
detached at the same time, and also that the detachment of
man should be an imitation of God's. But the imitation of
God is connected with our disposition of will in the same
way that our virtue has to be related to the disposition of our
gnome.[12] It is thus the natural energy of man that should be
liberated and used in imitation of God, even if it has to
cooperate with divine grace and manifest itself in communication with Christ, God and man.

This natural energy should be connected to the whole
composite phenomenon of man, his sensible and intelligible

[9]Cf. Ga. 3:28; *Patr. Gr.* 90, 993 B, trans. by P. Sherwood.
[10]On the Evagrian and Maximian understanding of detachment, cf.
Thunberg, *op. cit.,* pp. 319-327.
[11]*St. Maximus the Confessor: The Ascetic Life* . . . , p. 93.
[12]See *Letter 1*; *Patr. Gr.* 91, 364 AB.

elements, since only this totality is in accordance with the *logos* of human nature. Consequently, detachment must be more than just emptiness. In its negative aspect it is absence of evil passions; in its positive aspect it is connected also with a good—and active—use of man's faculties in virtue of his divine aim and in the service of charity. Maximus says that the *habitus* of detachment is a state in which "the face" of the psychic disposition of man is elevated in glorification of God, a "face" formed by a multitude and variety of virtues.[13]

We can now more easily understand why Maximus is never very interested in establishing a naked equilibrium of correspondences between vices and virtues, as Evagrius does. Rather he insists on the positive functions of the different faculties of the human soul as these may be developed in the plenitude of virtues.

Reintegration should take place in active charity, and therefore we must now turn our attention more directly and precisely to the function of charity at the different levels of Christian life.

CHARITY: THE SUPREME FACTOR OF INTEGRATION

This problem contains several aspects. Let us concentrate on three of them: (a) charity as the summit of all the virtues; (b) charity in its relation to faith and hope; and (c) the relationship between charity and knowledge (*gnosis*).

Charity as the Inclusive Summit of the Virtues

Frequently Maximus calls charity the most general or fundamental of virtues. But what is more important, he demonstrates that he regards the relationship between charity and the other virtues in a way different from that of Evagrius. In his *Letter 2,* he maintains that charity *possesses* or contains all the virtues. This means that, in a certain sense, some of the

[13]See *Quest. ad Thal* 54; *Patr. Gr.* 90, 512 A.

more "primitive" virtues no longer come to the fore, since
they are in a certain way replaced by charity. But this implication is very general and contains no evaluation of the virtues.
That is the other side of Maximus's position: no expression
or "form" of goodness is outside charity, according to Maximus, neither the other "theological" virtues, nor the virtues
of the *vita practica*. We are thus confronted with an inclusive
vision of charity as the perfection of virtuous life. Charity
adopts the other virtues into a more elevated unity and sup-
ports man with their vigor.

The virtues are natural, i.e. they are expressions of man's
true nature. This is Maximus's conviction. But charity is not
only natural. It is also a gift of God.[14] Here Maximus often
makes a distinction in his general conception of love between
natural desire (*eros*) and the divine gift (*agápe*), which is
charity, the supreme manifestation of God. Active charity in
the Christian is to Maximus always a theandric reality. It is
in that capacity that charity can also lead man beyond himself. Consequently, charity, the summit of the virtues, stands
in man in living communion with God's charity. It is a natural
desire sustained by divine charity, the fruit of which is divine-
human and at the same time the perfection of all that is in
man.[15]

This does not necessarily lead to the conclusion, however,
that charity is altogether a supernatural *habitus* in man. In
my opinion, charity is for Maximus a double reality, the
supreme manifestation of the theandric dimension both in
man *and* in God. It expresses precisely the reciprocity between
God and man that we dealt with in the last chapter. It is a
form of communion that includes all that is natural in man
and makes him communicate with the divine grace that
becomes manifest at the same time in that communication.[16]

Charity is always of a double character, which manifests
itself in its relationship with the three elements of the human
soul. The relationship between love of God and a good use

[14]On this aspect of charity in Maximus, cf. Garrigues, *op. cit.*, pp. 176-199.

[15]A valuable analysis of charity according to Maximus is given by
W. Völker, *op. cit.*, pp. 423-445.

[16]Cf. Garrigues on this synergy of charity, *op. cit.*, p. 188.

of man's concupiscible faculty is clearly expressed by Maximus. This is, by the way, one of the points where he comes close to St. Augustine. The relationship between love of neighbor and the good use of man's irascible faculty is indicated even more often. We find a characteristic statement in *Centuries on Charity*, I:66:

> The passions of the irascible part of the soul are naturally harder to oppose than those of the concupiscible. Therefore a better remedy against them was given by the Lord, the command of charity.[17]

But the two are certainly also combined, since God is love, and the demand for love is expressed in the *double* commandment. Thus Maximus writes in *Centuries on Charity*, I:38:

> If long-suffering and kindness belong to charity, the angry man and evil-doer is clearly made alien to charity; but being alien to charity is being alien to God, since *God is love.*[18]

Man's rational faculty is also related to the work of charity. In the first place, here we are dealing with love of God.[19] The activity of the mind in pure prayer is also, according to Maximus, an expression of the love of God. Maximus says: ". . . the man who loves God is concerned for pure prayer and he casts out of himself every passion that obstructs his way to it."[20]

We have thus seen that in Maximus's opinion the supreme virtue of charity integrates positively all the more "primitive" virtues by bringing them to their perfection. We have also seen that this positive evaluation of the virtues in relation to charity is closely linked with Maximus's evaluation of charity in its *two* aspects, implying a good use of the three faculties of the human soul in making it capable of final communion with God.

[17]*Patr. Gr.* 90, 973 C; trans. by Sherwood.
[18]*Patr. Gr.* 90, 968 B; trans. by Sherwood.
[19]See e.g. *Centuries on Charity; Patr. Gr.* 90, 976 A.
[20]*Ibid.,* II:7; *Patr. Gr.* 90, 985, BC.

But this means further that Maximus does not share the opinion of an Evagrius that man leaves his "passible" functions behind (i.e. his capacity for desire and engagement as a being both sensual and spiritual) during the process of deification and Christian perfection. Actually, charity implies that this "passibility" be restored from its perversion and transformed, and that it thus accompany man through all his life as a human being. For this reason Maximus is prepared to call charity itself *a blessed passion*. In restored man the evil passion of desire for the world is replaced by the good passion of charity for God and for neighbor.

But what is the relationship between charity and the other two "theological" virtues, faith and hope?

Charity—Faith—Hope

On the basis of 1 Co. 13:13, Maximus affirms the supremacy of charity in relation to the other "theological" virtues. This is no surprise. But there are in Maximus other more interesting traits.

A remarkable fact is his very high estimation of *faith*. Like Evagrius he sees faith as the basis and point of departure for Christian life as a whole. But Maximus goes further. To Evagrius faith is only a kind of natural and purified *gnosis*. To Maximus faith is a gift of grace, given in baptism, a power and a vocation. According to him faith gives a qualified knowledge of God and divine things. This knowledge is contrasted with sensual and external knowledge and is called an "unformed" (inner) Kingdom of God, though the Kingdom itself is a divinely formed faith.[21] That is to say that naked faith must be filled with the virtues, but it is nevertheless always the Kingdom of God in man which, as manifested, takes shape through good works, as the *scholion* to this passage puts it.[22] Consequently, we must regard the supremacy of charity in light of this high estimation of faith.

On *hope,* too, Maximus takes a position different from

---

[21]See *Quaest. ad Thal.* 33; ed. Laga-Steel, p. 229.
[22]*Ibid.,* p. 231.

that of Evagrius. The latter sees its function in terms of assurance and confirmation, but Maximus goes further. To him hope is placed on a more elevated level, as the strength (*fortitudo*) of the other two. This means that the three "theological" virtues form a kind of divine triad, where hope is found in the middle. They are all like fixed stars in a supreme formation.

This is confirmed by another of Maximus's considerations. He places these "theological" virtues in relation to one of his other favorite triads, *beginning—intermediary—end*. Faith is the beginning, and hope is the intermediary, but in fact their mutual relationship is more complicated than that. For Maximus believes that *faith,* being the beginning, is also linked to the intermediary and to the end. Man has always to begin over and over again, having no proper access to a perfect knowledge of divine things. *Hope* is related to the intermediary and to charity, which represents the end. It has an intermediary function because it indicates the object of faith and manifests the object of charity. But *charity* alone is fully connected with the end as the consummation of all.

Charity is related to the end in the sense that it alone attains to the final object of true desire.[23] But it is also the respose (*stásis*) of man's movement even beyond himself: it represents the final point in the anti-Origenist triad of Maximus (already spoken of above), becoming—motion—fixity (*genesis—kinesis—stásis*).

Let us quote a passage from *Letter 2* that illustrates this very well:

> Faith, which firmly establishes truth, is the basis of that which comes afterwards, I mean hope and charity. Hope gives strength to the extremes, I mean faith and charity, showing in itself what is to be believed and what is to be loved, and teaching that the course to the goal should go through hope itself. Charity, however, is their fulfillment embracing entirely the supreme desirable in its totality and providing for them the rest of their movement towards it. . . .[24]

[23]See *Letter 2*; *Patr. Gr.* 91, 396 C.
[24]*Patr. Gr.* 91, 396 B.

In accordance with this Maximus states that charity is the perfect enjoyment (*apólausis*) of that toward which faith and hope are striving. Charity alone provides participation in divine supernatural things.[25] Charity alone can lead man to mystical union.

This position of charity, however, also calls attention to the problem of the relationship between charity and knowledge, to which we now turn.

Knowledge and Charity

The final union into which man is brought by charity, in Maximus's opinion, lies above all knowledge. *Centuries on Charity* I:100 is an important text at this point:

> Placed in God, and inflamed with desire, it seeks first of all the grounds of His being, but finds no encouragement in what is proper to Him; for that indeed is impossible and forbidden alike to every created nature. But it does receive encouragement from His attributes—I mean to say from the things that concern His eternity, infinity, and immensity; from His goodness, wisdom, and His power that makes, governs, and judges His creatures. "And with regard to Him, this only is completely understandable—infinity" [quotation from Gregory Nazianzen]; and the very fact of knowing nothing is knowledge surpassing the mind, as the theologians Gregory and Denis have said somewhere.[26]

Here Maximus shows that intelligence, even if it is "placed in God" and filled with true desire for Him (i.e. concupiscence fully transformed or charity as desire), cannot penetrate into that which is God's own being because it is forbidden to every creature. Nevertheless, it finds encouragement in the

[25]See *Quaest. ad Thal.* 59; *Patr. Gr.* 90, 608 D; cf. *Ambigua* 7; 91, 1077 AB.

[26]*Patr. Gr.* 90, 981 D-984 A.

divine attributes, i.e. in that which God reveals of Himself. We thus observe that according to Maximus even the illuminated intelligence, in its pure desire of love for God, seeks something in God that it is not permitted to comprehend. In this same love it is yet given to man to be united with God. This union is thus above and beyond knowledge and intelligence.

In this way charity is in all respect superior. On its way to the most perfect illumination, being open to it, the soul should be supported by charity. From this point of view it may seem that charity, as the supporter, is inferior and knowledge superior. But this is only one aspect of a totality. The mind needs the support of charity precisely because charity is capable of bringing it beyond itself. In each text in which Maximus speaks of charity, the exact context should be observed.

Charity is thus on the one hand a fruit of the purification of passions, which makes the soul (*psychè*) joyful, and is something different from knowledge (*gnosis*), which is related to the mind (*nous*). On the other hand, it is through charity that knowledge of God becomes attached to the purified intellect. It is charity that prepares the mind for its advancement in knowledge. Knowledge thus depends on charity, and this dependence never ceases. On the contrary, it is charity alone, as we have seen, that opens the door to mystical union for man.

Generally one might say that Maximus emphasizes—according to the tradition of Evagrius—the "gnostic" character of human desire for God (i.e. man seeks to *know* God). At the same time he stresses the fact that it is charity which leads man to true knowledge and illumination, *and* that human knowledge of God can never be completed since what God is in Himself remains incomprehensible to man. Only attaching to God man's pure desire in perfect charity, which expresses itself in a kind of ecstacy (*ekstasis* meaning man's going outside or beyond himself), unites man totally with God.[27]

27On this theme, see further Thunberg, *op. cit.*, pp. 432-454; cf. also Völker, *op. cit.*, pp. 335-365.

We might thus add the following conclusion. Charity generously opens the natural-social dimension in its totality. It is a double phenomenon in the same way as the commandment of love is double. It implies the perfect unification of all that is naturally and positively human, as well as its transcendence, going beyond this dimension as such. It is a mysteriously theandric reality, human desire and a divine power, united in the divine-human reciprocity that is the decisive perspective of creation as a human phenomenon. In virtue of this reciprocity charity leads and accompanies man on the whole road of salvation. But for this reason, too, the natural-social dimension is itself a reflection, a perfect image, of the creative "philanthropy" of God.

This last fact, however, is also illustrated in Maximus by his personal exploration of the divine incarnation or embodiment in human virtues themselves. Therefore, this subject must be our last consideration in this chapter, since in this embodiment the natural-social dimension again obtains its own true content as divine image.

DIVINE EMBODIMENT IN HUMAN VIRTUES

Charity secures not only a unified movement toward God as the true goal of man, but also a good use of man's different natural faculties and a just relationship between all men who share the same nature.

Maximus preserves a perfect equilibrium in establishing a clear correspondence between the integrative function of charity as a unified movement toward God and the very act of self-differentiation through which Christ the Logos allows Himself to become embodied in the multitude of human virtues.

The work of integration through which man can serve God is at the same time, in Maximus's opinion, a continual "incarnation" of the Logos in humanity, differentiating and concretizing, as it were, the divine presence according to the created diversity of human life. This idea is not unique to

Maximus, but he developed it in a more energetic way than did his predecessors.[28]

Maximus affirms that the Logos "becomes massive" in the man of the *vita practica* (*praktikós*) through the modes (*trópoi*) of the virtues that are active there and is incarnated in them, but also says that in the spiritual life of man He becomes "thin," as He was in the beginning, God the Logos.[29] There is thus a double movement (downward and upward; cf. Maximus's reflections on Christ's ascension). Nevertheless, there can be no doubt that Christ is also present in the ascetic virtues of the *vita practica,* an active participation underlining the important correspondence and connection between the divine incarnation and the continual human process of sanctification and deification.

As a matter of fact, Maximus's doctrine at this point is very advanced. First of all, the grace of baptism implies an inhabitation of Christ in the Christian. Secondly, faith becomes the mother of the Logos in man. The Logos is the son of faith in the sense that He incarnates Himself on the basis of faith through practiced virtues.[30] It is in its capacity as the source of virtues that faith becomes the mother of the Logos. Maximus regards this presence as a kind of incarnation.

Further, according to Maximus, the purification of the passions prepares for the experience of a presence of Christ. In reality, the Logos is present both through virtues and through knowledge. Substantially—and here Maximus is in accord with a number of his predecessors—the virtues are Christ, and this fact is explicitly understood as a divine incarnation in the virtuous life of man. There is also a link between this moral incarnation of Christ the Logos and the presence communicated through knowledge (*gnosis*), i.e. contemplation through reason and intellect. As a matter of fact, there is also a correspondence between the two manners of presence, for it is through the *logoi* of the commandments that the Logos communicates with man in the *vita practica,* in the

---

[28]See Thunberg, *op. cit.,* pp. 342-350.
[29]See *Gnost.* 2:37; *Patr. Gr.* 90, 1141 C.
[30]See *Quaest. ad Thal.* 40; *Patr. Gr.* 90, 400 BC.

same way as it is through the *logoi* of things as subjects of contemplation that He communicates in the process of *gnosis*. Those who keep the commandments are morally in communion with the Logos, developing their natural virtues as Christian virtues. These virtues make sense precisely through the correspondence between the *logos* of human nature, in accordance with which they are natural virtues, and the Logos Christ, present in virtuous Christians.

However, moral communion with the Logos is closely related to the intellectual comprehension of this principle (*logos*) of nature. Christ incarnates Himself in the virtues of the believer, but the believer also elevates himself, through contemplation and insight, to a comprehension more elevated than all the commandments, a comprehension, although limited, of the unique source of all the principles and laws, all the *logoi*, the Logos, and God Himself.

We have seen that Maximus believes that Christ is present in man's *vita practica,* but also that the human intellect, letting itself be unified with God, contains, in a moral sense, divine attributes as they are reflected in him through virtue. In light of the divine-human reciprocity we see how divine attributes and human virtues (which are natural in so far as they are in accordance with the *logos* of human nature) correspond mutually in the same sense as the incarnation of Christ and the deification of man correspond. The relationship between the virtues, corresponding to the divine commandments, and the revealed attributes of God is modeled on the hypostatic relationship between the human and the divine in Christ.

This is precisely what Maximus affirms in *Letter 2,* where he says that deifying charity permits a *reciprocal attribution* (*antidosis schetikè*) between those who are being united, i.e. God and man, in a communication (*communicatio idiomatum*) similar to that between the two natures in Christ. Maximus writes:

> For the most perfect work of charity and the culmination of its activity is to attain, through a reciprocal attribution, that the attributes of those whom it unites

pass from one to the other, and likewise the names of
these qualities, and that it makes man act and appear
as God, through the one and unchangeable decision
and motion of will on both sides, such as we see it in
Abraham and the other saints. And this is perhaps what
is said about the person of God: "In the hands of the
prophets I have made myself similar" [Hos. 12:10]
to express how God, through the unitive practice of
virtue, makes Himself conform with everyone due to
His great love for human beings. For the "hand" of
every just person is His virtuous practice—in which and
through which God receives likeness unto men.[31]

The christological convictions of the councils of Chalcedon
and Constantinople (of the years 451 and 553) are here transferred to the level of the virtues in the sense that human
integration and unification, established through a correct relation to God as goal, is maintained and confessed to the same
extent that human differentiations are also maintained,
through an act of divine-human mutual appropriation. The
natural-social dimension is thus not neglected but affirmed
precisely within the relationship in which it is transcended.
Such a dialectic is characteristic of Maximus.

In order not to forget the social aspect of this dimension,
however, in reference also to Maximus's admirable skill in
keeping all things together in his vision, let us end this
chapter with another quotation, one dealing with love for
one's neighbor. It is taken from *Liber Asceticus* 8:

For those who are created after the image of God and
are motivated by reason [logos, with reference to
man as a rational being, but through this also to the
logos of his nature, common to all mankind], who
are thought worthy of knowledge of God and receive
their law from Him, it is possible not to repulse those
who cause them grief and to love those who hate
them. Hence when the Lord says: "Love your enemies;
do good to them that hate you," he does not command

[31]*Patr. Gr.* 91, 401 B.

the impossible, but clearly what is possible; for He would not otherwise rebuke the transgressor. The Lord Himself makes it clear and has shown it to us by His very works; and so too all His disciples, who strove till death for love of their neighbor and prayed fervently for those who killed them. But since we are lovers of material things and of pleasure, preferring them above the commandment, we are not then able to love those who hate us, being worse disposed than beasts and creeping things. And that is why, not being able to follow in the steps of God, we are likewise unable to know His purpose, so that we might receive strength.

We find in this text a number of the ingredients of Maximus's thinking as we have dealt with them in this chapter: a reference to the correspondence between the divine purpose for man and the *logos* of his being, emphasis on the connection between the two sides of the commandment of love, stress on Christ as a model, a combination of virtue and true knowledge, and finally the virtues being expressions of god-like behavior.

CHAPTER 6

The Liturgical and Sacramental Dimension

This last chapter on the different dimensions of Maximus's theology deals in fact with *ecclesiology,* since the ecclesiology of Maximus, with some exceptions, is in principle of a liturgical and sacramental nature. And—this is an important addition—ecclesiology is for him more a dimension than a specified theme of theology (this may be due to his being a layman—a historical problem not yet solved); at any rate, it includes, and is dominated by, his understanding of the liturgy and the sacraments.

To Maximus the Church is not an ecclesiastical institution distributing divine grace, but truly a Mystical Body that represents symbolically the whole divine-human mystery, the whole mystery of God's good counsel, and the economy of salvation. One might even say that ecclesiology in this sense is not only one of the dimensions but *the supreme* dimension. It contains the total vision of Maximus, a vision that is altogether liturgical and sacramental at the same time. It was not by chance that Hans Urs von Balthasar labeled his great study of Maximus *The Cosmic Liturgy.*

It is especially in the *Mystagogia* (a work whose date is uncertain but which probably dates from Maximus's stay in Carthage since in its ascetical and exegetical aspects it comes close to the *Liber Asceticus* and the *Questions to Thalassius*) that Maximus develops his mystical ecclesiology. It is characteristic that he does this in a piece that is formally an

113

explanation of the eucharistic liturgy, especially the *Synaxis*. There are essential comments that are missing, e.g. an explication and interpretation of the Anaphora, but it is beyond doubt that to Maximus the celebration of the eucharist by the people of God is the symbolic and sacramental center of the whole Christian existence as well as of the Church.

In his commentary on this feast of the Lord, he gathers together in an admirable way all his essential considerations regarding the soteriological mysteries, especially those of creation, incarnation, the ascetic life and the mystical communion (understood for preference in monastic terms), *and* the mystery of deifying consummation. It is in this presupposed structure of worship and it is also before this altar invisibly present in his text that he places all the truths of his theological cosmos. His speculation on the "mysteries" of the Church are thus rooted in daily eucharistic reality, but they do not stop there in any superficial way. This same reality is for him a true mystery, i.e. an effective and totally inclusive symbol, which has the purpose of bringing us—in a sense he calls "anagogical"—all the way to the most elevated mysteries, to the very goal of our spiritual life.

Two more remarks should be made. Maximus probably makes these comments as a layman and at the same time as a monk. The fact that he is a layman may explain his silence about the Anaphora (the Eucharistic Prayer). We shall return to that problem in the Appendix. Anyway, his comments do not reflect the attitude of a priest. At the time of Maximus the words of the Anaphora were already covered by a low intonation; Maximus concentrates his attention on those elements of the liturgy that were open to any participant. But this also means that for him, probably experiencing the eucharistic celebration from the point of view of a lay participant, *the culmination of the whole liturgy is in the communion.* About the latter he expressed himself in the following way:

> . . . as a consummation of everything the distribution of the mystery takes place. It transforms in itself and renders those who participate worthily, through grace

and participation, similar to the Good which is the Cause. They lack nothing of it so far as it is available and possible to attain for men. In this way they may both be and be called gods through the gift of grace, since God as a whole fills them entirely and does not let any part of them be empty of His presence.[1]

At this point an observation of Fr. René Bornert ought to be mentioned.[2] Bornert points out that Maximus—even though his expressed intention in the *Mystagogia* is to give an "anagogical" interpretation—tends to replace the terms *typikos* (by type) and *mystikos* (mystically, i.e. in reality spiritually) with the terms *genikos* (in general) and *idikos* (in particular). The explanation of Fr. Bornert is the following: "The general history of salvation, dealing with humanity as a totality, becomes, through the mediation of the liturgical celebration, a particular and special history concerning each member of the people of God." If this observation is correct, it is precisely this link between what is "general" in the reality of the Church and its individual, mystical, and total consummation in divinization, which the eucharistic liturgy offers and represents. Maximus's ecclesiology is not individualizing—quite to the contrary. The aim of its "symbolical" mediation is precisely this realization, in the mystical and theandric Body of Christ without divisions, of one's own destiny—and, one could add, of the destiny of man as "monk" (i.e. a person who is alone, who lives *monadikos*). It would, however, be false to presuppose at this point any grave tension between what is general and what is individual: the individual realization of the aim of man *is* the manifestation of this aim as common to all mankind, and cannot be otherwise.

That Maximus wrote his commentary on the liturgy as a monk also means that he wrote it as a disciple, an inheritor of a long tradition of monastic wisdom and experience. All his predecessors in this tradition are not easily identified, but two figures seem to be more impotrant than the others: Pseudo-Dionysius the Areopagite (whose *Ecclesiastical Hier-*

---

[1]*Mystagogia* 21; *Patr. Gr.* 91, 697 A.
[2]See *Studia patristica* 10, 1976, p. 327.

archy serves him as an explicit model) and that anonymous "old man," whose wise teaching Maximus says that he only wants to convey. If this latter person really existed and is not a literary fiction—and we are here confronted with the same kind of problem as in the case of the old monk in the *Liber Asceticus*—he was probably that abbot Sophronius, whom Maximus met and lived with in Carthage and who became the anti-monoenergetic Patriarch of Jerusalem (see chapter 1 above). Whatever the influence of this man, however, one should not underestimate the importance of the *Mystagogia* as a profound expression of Maximus's own theology.[3]

It is thus meaningful to concentrate our attention in this chapter on certain aspects of Maximus's ecclesiology as they are developed in his *Mystagogia*. The structure of that work dictates our own structure, even though our interest here is particularly concentrated on the first chapters, where Maximus gives his visionary definitions of what in his view the Church truly is. (In the Appendix, I will deal with other parts of the *Mystagogia*.)

THE CHURCH AS A FIGURE OF GOD

This is the theme of chapter 1 of the *Mystagogia*. If we may look upon this work as a kind of synthesis of Maximus's thinking, we are also entitled to interpret what is said here as its fundamental basis.

Maximus starts with the following statement of his subject: "To what extent and how the holy Church is the image and figure of God." He continues by giving a summary of his theology of creation, where he works once more with his fundamental distinction between the *principle of essence/ nature* (*logos ousias/physeos*) and the *mode of existence* (*tropos hyparxeos*). This distinction implies that in the created world there is not only a fixity of created natures or species in their diversity but also a "tropical" movement that is to

---

[3]On Sophronius of Jerusalem, see further the important presentation by Fr. Chr. Schönborn, O.P., *Sophrone de Jérusalem. Vie Monastique et confession dogmatique*, Paris 1972.

lead to a unification of all the principles (*logoi*) in their final Cause (God as the Creator of all that is). This movement of realization corresponds to the descending movement of God in the acts of creation and soteriological providence.

Thus, what Maximus describes is the Church as representative of creation as a totality, the Church of all the nations and all the peoples. The Church consists of different persons who, in their multiplicity, represent the multiplicity of the created universe. The problem here, however, is how the Church can also be an icon of God. Maximus's answer to this question could finally be formulated in the following way: *The Church is an icon of God in virtue of its communion in "tropical" energy with Him.*

The energy that makes all its individuals into the Church, the Body of Christ, is the unifying energy that is the image of the uni-diversifying energy of God. He is the only cause of all that is, and as Cause He is also the principle of unity.

When, in the Church, the created multiplicity assembles around Christ, who is the only *logos* of the totality—assembles without confusion, but also without separation between the divine and the human, as the Chalcedonian formula states— then the Church expresses in a "typical" mode (i.e. as type) one and the same principle and one and the same power of unity on the level of creation. This now happens, Maximus says, by *imitation,* since there is no identity of essence, and by *imprint* (type), since it is not the Archetype Himself who is involved. There can be no doubt that St. Paul's vision of the Church as one body with many members has exercised a decisive influence on this vision.

Two quotations might close this section of our presentation. Both are from chapter 1 of the *Mystagogia.* The first of them describes the Church as an icon of God:

> The Holy Church is thus, as stated, an icon of God in that it accomplishes the same unity among the believers as God. However different they are by their characteristics and their differences of place and ways of life, they find themselves nevertheless unified in it through faith.

This unity was accomplished by God in regard to the essences of beings without confusion, in bringing into silence and "same-ness" what there is of difference, as has been demonstrated, through their tendency toward Him and their unification with Him as Cause and Ground and Goal.[4]

The second text is from an earlier section of the same chapter and describes the Christ-likeness of the Church:

To all it (the Church) offers as a grace in equal manner one unique divine form and appellation, that of being and being named from Christ.

It gives them a unique relationship in faith which is simple and undivided and without the differences between them, which exist in great number and which are impossible to mention not even taking notice of their existence, and it does so by bringing all and uniting all to itself in a "catholic" way.[5]

There is, however, another aspect of the Church, too, and this is treated in the second and third chapters of the *Mystagogia.*

THE CHURCH AS AN IMAGE OF THE WORLD

In the chapter on the theandric dimension we noticed that one of the five mediations of man and of Christ as his representative, i.e. the fourth mediation, is that between sensible and intelligible creation. We have also seen that in Maximus's thinking the microcosmic situation of man is precisely based on the fact that he alone is by constitution both a sensual and intellectual being at the same time. This duality (without dissolution) of creation is the dominant aspect in the second chapter of the *Mystagogia.* The third

[4]*Myst.* I; *Patr. Gr.* 91, 668 BC.
[5]*Patr. Gr.* 91, 665 CD.

chapter considers the meaning of the Church as visible and sensible creation.

To better understand what Maximus wants to say on this subject, we should repeat the most essential points of his thoughts on the fourth mediation. First of all, we must not forget that the two forms of human life are, in Maximus's opinion, both of them, truly created forms. Second, this mediation was effected by Christ in His ascension through the angelic orders as true man, in soul and in body. Third, through this act Christ reveals a tendency that is common to the whole of creation, i.e. to become coordinated in a non-divided totality. Fourth, this revelation implies that there is in fact one common *logos* for the whole of creation, and finally, that man should carry this mediation out through a knowledge similar to that of the angels. All these themes now represent the background for what Maximus says in the *Mystagogia.*

Yet, first he reflects on the Church as a particular building when he says that it constitutes an image of this dual world.

> It is divided into a separated space, reserved for the priests and liturgical servants alone, which we call the sanctuary, and a space which is accessible to all believing people, which we name the nave. Yet it is one according to *hypostasis*.[6]

Here we are confronted with a very simple kind of symbolism. But there is more to say, for already the division described is a division on two levels, that of Church architecture and that of liturgical ministers and actions. As a division it is precisely of an exterior and architectural character, but as a dual unity the Church also becomes manifest in its human and liturgical reality. We already know—and Maximus has underlined this in his first chapter—that the Church as a people constitutes a unity. Peopled by the Christians as a pluriform body, the Church building itself expresses its unity, and this unity is confirmed by the liturgy. This latter is also pluriform in a hierarchical sense, but the whole cele-

[6]*Patr. Gr.* 91, 668 D.

brating people celebrate it together. This in itself indicates precisely this tendency in creation which was revealed by Christ in His fourth mediation, a tendency that is confirmed by the unity of the theandric *hypostasis*. The word *hypostasis* in our quotation (which as to its subject is not yet christological) reminds us of that.

The text can be properly interpreted only through a correct apprehension of what man is. Chapter 2 is complementary to chapter one. Maximus draws attention to the fact that the Church belongs to the created world and thus reflects the world in its own constitution. It consists of men who are themselves divided into two categories. Men may get to know creation in a double manner that corresponds to their own double constitution: sensibly through the senses and intelligibly through their mind and their rational faculty. And yet it is the same world. What the senses experience may be used symbolically in reference to the spiritual truth about all that is. The intellectual comprehension of creation concerns the same reality. Analogically and symbolically one may get access to the truth about things through *exterior* impressions and through an *interior* communication between the *logos* of man, his reasonable faculty, and the *logoi* of things, their ruling principles. The human intellect may at one and the same time gain comprehension of the same visible and invisible creation. Duality not only constitutes a separation but also a parallelism within creation.

In the same way, in the liturgy of the Church one may learn the spiritual truths both symbolically through the exterior forms of the liturgical action and at the same time through direct communion at the altar. (On the problem of communion and real presence see, below, the Appendix.) The truth is the same, and comprehended in this way it also indirectly reflects the Church in heaven.

We may sum up with two quotations. The first one concerns contemplation and the second the indirect, iconic, relationship with divine realities. On symbolic contemplation Maximus seems to say that it is only secondary to pure contemplation, which does not pass through sensible visualizations, since that has, as it were, immediate access to the *logoi* of things. Nevertheless, symbolic contemplation is a proper contemplation. Maximus expresses it in a very sophisticated way:

> Symbolic contemplation of intelligible things through the visible is a spiritual understanding and insight of visible things through the invisible.[7]

Thus it is no surprise that the Church, while being an image of the world, yet seen from above or from the interior, also gives an indication of the heavenly reality and its liturgical celebration. Maximus says:

> It is another kind of Church, not made by hands which is wisely revealed by that which is made by hands and which possesses in the form of sanctuary the superior world attributed to the powers above, and as nave the one below reserved for those who participate in sensible life.[8]

In chapter 3 Maximus adds, without committing himself to it, another possible symbolism: the Church is also an image of the sensible world as such. Here, however, the symbolism is itself reciprocal. The Church as world has its sanctuary as heaven and its nave as earth, but one may also say that the world is a church having heaven as its sanctuary and earth as its nave. This means that what really concerns Maximus is the superiority of an ecclesial vision of the world. The world itself is a church, and this fact implies by consequence the possibility of the first symbolism: the relationship of the Church with the world as both sensible and intelligible. Thus, to Maximus the Church is never separated from the world as cosmos. It represents it and includes it through its own constitution as a building and its own activity as people of God, its symbolism being a reflection of a double reality in which it participates, the purpose of which it communicates as a spiritual reality in Christ.

[7]*Myst.* 2; *Patr. Gr.* 91, 669 CD.
[8]*Ibid.,* 669 AB.

But thereby a road is open to further symbolism, which is directly anthropological, and this is what concerns Maximus in chapter 4 of his *Mystagogia*.

THE CHURCH AS MAN AND
MAN AS CHURCH

Here reciprocity is presented at the very outset: Man and Church reflect and symbolize each other reciprocally. Maximus's method of interpretation is more clearly allegorical at this point.

Here the Pauline trichotomy (St. Paul speaks of man as consisting of body, soul, and spirit) is also inscribed in the system. This means that the Church as a building is now seen as divided into three parts, organized according to their sacredness: to the spirit corresponds the altar, to the soul the sanctuary, and to the body the nave. But what is important for Maximus is precisely the reciprocity between them: the Church reflects man in his constitution as the latter reflects and represents the Church in man. Man is in fact a church in the world, and the Church is universal Man, what Maximus calls the *makranthropos*.

Consequently in Maximus's view around man, as the microcosmic center of creation and the key to its interpretation, there are gathered all the created realities, anthropologically organized to be the Church of God. But man as the key also represents the goal of all this creation: he is the motive force who, in humanizing the realities around him, brings them to their true realization through being in the image and likeness of God. For this reason, the Church as man (anthropologically interpreted) is itself the image and likeness of God. Maximus writes: "[The Church] is in the image and likeness of man created in the image and likeness of God."[9]

The reciprocity can thus result in a spiritual activity, in which all the stages of Christian life are carried out. Maximus continues:

[9]*Ibid.*, 672 B.

. . . man is a mystical church. Through his body as
nave he illumines the practical life of his soul through
the energies of the commandments in accordance with
the moral philosophy; through the sanctuary of his
soul he brings to God, through "natural" contemplation and reason, the sensible *logoi* as purely detached
in the spirit from matter; and through the altar of
his spirit he invokes the silence full of hymns of praise,
the silence of the invisible and unknown great voice of
Divinity . . .[10]

Much more detailed, however, is Maximus's description of
the Church as an image of the soul, considered in itself,
which we find in chapter 5 of the *Mystagogia*.

THE CHURCH AS AN IMAGE OF
THE HUMAN SOUL

Chapter 5 of the *Mystagogia* is comparatively long.
The reason for this is that Maximus obviously had the intention of presenting a whole psychology of his own. One might
ask why he does this, but even if we consider it a digression
from the main line of his argument, we should notice the
significance of the analogy that he wants to establish. What
particular aspect of his ecclesiology is it that he wants to underline here? This is, after all, relatively clear. As Fr. Riou has
well expressed it, the significance is that the Church "realizes
in its parts the same unification that the soul exerts in
relation to its faculties."[11]

Our primary interest here is, therefore, not to enter into
the psychological details but to present an understanding of
the ruling tendencies and principles of Maximus's psychology.
Here follows a summary of important aspects.

One most essential thing is, of course, the fundamental
dichotomy in man: he is at the same time an intelligible and
a sensible being. This fact has a decisive influence on the

[10]*Ibid.*, 672 BC.
[11]*Op. cit.*, p. 153.

soul, which is situated in between the two extremes. As a matter of fact the soul is characterized by its double relationship. It receives sensations from the external world and builds on them in forming an image of the world, but it knows also, through its rational nature if it is not disturbed by passionate attachments to sensible things, the principles (*logoi*) of things and is thus capable of forming through them a more accurate image of the world.

These two kinds of images, however, represent one and the same world, and the task of the soul as mediator is to coordinate them ("from above," certainly) into one single totality. The idea is allegorically verbalized by Maximus in *Questions to Thalassius,* no. 40, in connection with the marriage in Cana. Here he says that the human soul should be made one with virtue as its bride, a unity that the Logos, born by faith, then honors with His presence.[12] The symbiosis between the two parts of man is effected by a soul that is regulated according to the principle of its nature, its *logos physeos,* and a soul that receives in virtue of this rectification the presence of the Logos with itself. This type of symbolism obviously forms a kind of basis for Maximus's reflections on the Church as soul.

For him the two forces of the soul, the power of vitality and the intellectual power, should both be harmonized through the natural tendency of the totality of human existence. The natural movements of the soul, prescribed by God, do not divide the human composite unity, but vitalize it in an effective manner in order to realize the image and likeness of God. In the *vita practica* and the *vita contemplativa* (seen as parallel expressions of man as being organized and harmonized according to his nature), the totality of that which is man expresses itself according to its divine principle (*logos*).

In the chapter 5 of the *Mystagogia* Maximus emphasizes especially the parallel movements of the mind (*nous*) and reason (the *logos* in its limited sense). The mind (*nous*) directs the gnostic activity of man, whose goal is truth, giving him access to true spiritual goods. At the same time reason

12See ed. Laga-Steel, p. 273.

directs the activity of the *practical life,* the end of which in rational beings is virtue as the basis of faith. Here, finally, we find the analogy of the Church. Maximus again calls our attention to the division of the Church building into sanctuary and nave, representing the duality of the human soul.

A conclusion may be presented in the form of a quotation from the fifth chapter of the *Mystagogia,* thus explaining this fundamental aspect of Maximus's ecclesiology. For Maximus, Man and Church have one and the same goal. The Church is seen in terms of his sharing in the common human destiny the Church is responsible for. In fact, the two realities coincide, for man is a Church and the Church is a man:

> Those are, as has been said, the parts of the soul. According to its mind [*nous*] it possesses wisdom, from wisdom it arrives at contemplation, from that to knowledge [*gnosis*], from that to the unforgettable gnosis, and through that it is brought to truth which is the end and the goal of all the good things of the mind [*nous*]. According to its reason it possesses prudence, from that it arrives at practice, and from practice to virtue, and from that again to faith according to which it reposes in the good as the blessed end of all reasonable activities. Through them the understanding of divine things is put together, according to the coming together in the union of these things in relation to one another. It is to all these things that the Church adapts itself clearly, being compared with the soul in contemplation. Through the sanctuary it signifies all that manifests itself in the mind and out of the mind [*nous*]. Through the nave it makes certain the things which appear according to reason and out of reason. And it brings all to its fulfillment in the mystery of the divine altar. All that can be explained through what is being performed in the Church makes quite clear that man's own soul is really a Church and divine. It may be because of this that the Church which is made by hands, on account of the variety of divine things in it, is a symbolic

model and has been given to us as a guide toward the excellent good.[13]

As we notice, the Church as an image of the created world can only point through its symbolism to the ultimate truth, since this truth is found in mystical union beyond all mediated knowledge. But the Church also undoubtedly opens up the final route to this union, since it is the place where the deifying grace of God is at work among men. For, as Maximus expressed it in chapter 6 of his *Mystagogia,* "the Church is a spiritual man and man is a mystical Church."[14]

At this point, then, the rites of the eucharist in its proper sense also have an important role to play as an indication of the consummation that is to come. In chapter 16 of the *Mystagogia* Maximus says, for example, that the "Great Entry" with the eucharistic gifts "begins and inaugurates the future apocalypse of the Mystery of our salvation which is hidden in impenetrable divine secrecy,"[15] and in chapter 17 he says that the kiss of peace prefigures and describes beforehand the future reconciliation of all rational beings in the one Logos. Yet, it is especially, as Fr. Riou points out,[16] "in the communion, the summit of the liturgy and of the mystical life, that we find a profoundly mystical, and not only an anticipatory and representative, preoccupation" with things divine. Holy communion is thus conceived as a sacramental integration of the whole human person before and toward its final and ultimate goal, which is the Trinitarian God Himself, the image and likeness of whom it carries and manifests. To this last aspect we shall return in more detail in the Appendix.

Thus we may conclude that Maximus sees the Church (as building and as people) both in a symbolical and a realistic perspective, and that for him there is no decisive tension between these two perspectives. The same observation can be made regarding the sacraments. They are symbols, and as

[13]*Patr. Gr.* 91, 681 C-684 A.
[14]*Ibid.,* 684 A.
[15]*Myst.* 16; *Ibid.,* 693 C.
[16]*Op. cit.,* p. 167.

such they may be allegorically interpreted, but they are also a reality that transforms the life of Christians through divine grace. This all depends on Maximus's understanding of the created world. That understanding can best be termed a sacramental one. On account of the presence of the Logos in all things, holding their *logoi* together, the world is pregnant with divine reality, and knowledge of it—through the rational quality of man, his own *logos*—is itself a kind of communion with God, a participation in divine things through the aims and purposes that are recognized in creation.

What happens in the Divine Liturgy is both symbol and reality at the same time. The liturgical acts have—precisely as symbols—a representative character; they participate in the divine reality as secrets and mysteries to be interpreted by the believing mind. Thus, liturgical sharing in these divine things also prefigures and represents the ongoing, and possible, divinization of man.

A quotation from chapter 23 of the *Mystagogia* may illustrate this:

> Having received—in a dignity like unto that of the holy angels—the luminous *logoi* concerning Divinity, as far as they are accessible to creation, and having learned to laud the unique Divinity, without ever keeping silence and in symphony with the angels, in a trinitarian manner, the soul is brought through close resemblance into the filiation of grace. Through that, and carrying in its prayer its God as the unique mystical Father according to grace, it will gather itself together, through an ecstacy outside of everything toward the One who is its secrecy. It will sense and know all the more the divine mysteries as it will not be of itself, nor be known itself through itself or by another person but received by the entire God, who brings it entirely to the good, entirely present in it in a divine manner and penetrating into it without passion, deifying it entirely. In this way, as the totally saintly Dionysius the Areopagite says, it becomes the icon and the manifestation of invisible light, an immaculate

mirror, most transparent, complete, immaculate, un-
contaminated, receiving into itself entirely the splen-
dor of the type of Goodness and radiating in a godlike
manner without restrictions, as far as that is possible,
the Goodness of the silence of inaccessible places.[17]

In another text of similar interest, Maximus comments
on the secret things related to the Christian life seen as a
sacramental life. I refer to the so-called *Gnostic Centuries*
I:37 ff., where Maximus deals with the interpretation of the
Sabbath and matters connected with the Sabbath: true circumcision, eschatological harvest, etc. It becomes clear, that
the prescriptions of the Old Covenant, allegorically, also have
their very deep Christian significance, and that this significance
is, in a broad sense, sacramental in character.

37. The Sabbath is the detachment [*apatheia*]
of the rational soul, having totally rejected the marks
[*stigmata*] of sin through practice.

38. The Sabbaths signify the liberty of the rational
soul having laid aside its natural energy toward the
sensible world.

39. The Sabbath of Sabbaths is the spiritual tranquil-
ity of the rational soul, having brought its mind away
from the most divine principles [*logoi*] of beings,
entirely attached to God alone through an ecstacy of
desire, and being itself entirely immobile in God
through mystical theology.

40. Circumcision is the putting away of the tendency
of the soul to be affected by what is coming into
being [*genesis*].

41. The circumcision is the total rejection and denial
of the natural movements of the soul in relation to
the future.

42. The harvest is for the rational soul the gathering

[17]*Myst.* 23; *Patr. Gr.* 91, 701 BC; the translation is influenced by the
interpretation of Fr. Riou, *op. cit.*, p. 167.

together and the understanding with insight of the more spiritual principles [*logoi*] as to virtue and nature.

43. The harvest of harvests is the comprehension of God, inaccessible to all, beyond the mystical contemplation of intelligible things, in a manner inaccessible to the intellect.[18]

Through a spiritual interpretation, both of Scripture and of the liturgy, man on his spiritual journey may thus, according to Maximus, acquire access to a deeper communication with God, as being both the Creator of all that is and the hidden Lord of the insights of the mind, when it embarks upon an ecstatic journey beyond itself.

Like the other dimensions that we have considered, the liturgical and sacramental dimension is, as a matter of fact, a decisive dimension of life as a whole and cannot be neglected by any Christian. At the same time Maximus continues in a monastic tradition, which is inclined to see sacramental life as an expression of ascetic and spiritual life rather than as its source and instigation. In Maximus's mind, monastic life, with its examples of spiritual development and perfection, is always present, seeking its symbolic expressiveness in sacramental and liturgical reality.

[18]*Patr. Gr.* 90, 1097 C-1100 A.

CHAPTER 7

Further Reflections on Maximus's Theology

In the preceding chapters we have described the theology of Maximus the Confessor in terms of various dimensions. Through this method some elements have been treated at certain length and in some detail, while other elements have had to be left out. One such neglected field is Maximus's christology, considered in its more detailed points of view, and another is his mystical theology, which we have only hinted at.

This final chapter—and also the Appendix—has the function of supplementing at certain points what has been already considered. This does not mean that it will give a summary. Nor does it mean that the relevance of Maximus's theology for today will be adequately treated. My intention in this chapter is more limited. All readings and all interpretations of texts from the early Church demand a hermeneutical attitude that is always open to dialogue between these writers and the problems and questions put to us today. For this purpose both distance and proximity are important. The five "dimension" chapters above might have given enough proximity to allow a certain distance to mark out the profile of Maximus within a wider tradition of theology and in relation to the questions of our time.

The reflections that I propose here thus emerge from my many years of reading Maximus. I will concentrate my attention on three basic themes, mutually interrelated and yet,

131

each of them, rightfully claiming attention in itself. These reflections are of a somewhat personal character.

The first problem concerns the ontological perspective in Maximus: i.e. his reflections on the principles (*logoi*) of creation as seen in relation to some observations on the natural sciences of our own time. The second problem is that of the relationship between Maximus's theology and Eastern Orthodox Palamism (the tradition stemming from Gregory Palamas), seen as an invitation to ecumenical dialogue between the churches of East and West. The last problem is that of Maximus's eschatology: what did Maximus think about the end of time and about eternal life, and what can we learn today from his manner of resolving these intricate problems?

THE PRINCIPLES OR IDEAS OF CREATION AND NATURAL SCIENCE TODAY

Before Maximus, Christian thought about the Logos and the *logoi* of things had quite a history of its own. The christology of the prologue to the Gospel of St. John was quickly developed further in the ancient Church, especially in the theological school of Alexandria, and not only in explicit relation to a philosophical speculation of Stoic origin. It was also related to the Jewish theology of a Philo of Alexandria, even though some of the Fathers distinguished themselves from him at certain points. The Christian conviction that the identification of Jesus Christ and the Logos would imply a more elevated evaluation of Christ than that which Philo's thought would suggest was the main reason for this divergence. For, as a matter of fact, Philo did not consider the Logos as divine in the proper sense of the word, or at least only in a primary phase, while in a secondary phase He was created by God.[1]

A number of ancient Christian writers, however, made use of the Philonian understanding of the Logos as the ideal and true center of the intelligible world. This corresponds

[1]On Philo's speculations, see e.g. Jean Daniélou, *Philon d'Aléxandrie*, Paris 1958.

to a totality of ideas in a Platonic sense, but there is a difference. Philo as a Jew sees the Logos in terms of a personal Deity, and thus the coming together of all the ideas in the Logos means their coming together in God. But what is the relationship between God and His Logos as the principle of the created world? Here is the point where the Christian writers claimed that they had another answer than that of Philo, thanks to their Trinitarian theology. The Logos as the Second Person in the Godhead holds all things together in Himself. All that is created is created according to divine intention, the subject of which is the personal Logos, who entered this world in history and became man to fulfill the purpose of creation and of man as its microcosm. This at least is the line of thinking that Maximus follows. But this means, then, that the whole creation is filled with the divine presence. This is a presence that is not only of an abiding quality but also has a purpose and an aim to be carried out through man's free acceptance of it.

In general, the ancient writers also had the conviction that—thanks to the decisive act of creation—this world of ideas, aims, purposes, and principles is present in the concrete and observable world of creation. Through Christ, the Logos, this world, not only as an intelligible world, but also, often, as a sensible world, was in their view related to God through its capacity of being the outward manifestation of His own ideas. Through this very qualified Christian adaptation of the Philonian identification between the Logos and the Platonic world of ideas, the Fathers of the Church were able to arrive at an evaluation of creation that was a combination of the Biblical view of God's creation and Hellenistic speculation, a view open to the understanding of Christ as the Mediator of the Universe. Because of this, the theological understanding of the world was from then on linked by necessity to the development of the central doctrines of christology.

It is precisely at this point that we meet Maximus. His speculation about the created world represents an advance in christological reflection on the created order. Of his predecessors Origen was the first to develop a kind of theology of the *logoi* of creation. We might notice a similar trend in St.

Athanasius and, for that matter, also in St. Augustine. For the latter, the *rationes* (the Latin translation of *logoi*) are the immutable and eternal principles held together in the Logos. The most important influence, however, exerted upon Maximus came from Evagrius Ponticus and his school. Maximus was confronted by this school when he became a monk. It gave him a spiritual guidance that he would never reject, even though his faithfulness to Chalcedonian christology helped him to establish distance from some of the theological sidetracking of this tradition. Evagrius not only considered the *logoi* of creation in the same way as Origen, but also, as we have seen, he takes into account the *logoi* of providence and judgment, which are related to the *logoi* of creation. This fact makes the problem of the relationship between creation and salvation relevant to Maximus, and he struggles with it intensely, as we have already seen. Evagrius also proposed a final "spiritual contemplation" of all the *logoi*, in which they may be seen in their mystical communion with God. The other important predecessor is Pseudo-Dionysius the Areopagite, who regarded the *logoi* not only as more or less static ideas of God lying behind creation, but also in a dynamic sense as "divine and good intentions" for the world, almost identical with their possible forms of existence.

To Maximus, the *logoi* are precisely the divine intentions. This understanding of them is closely connected to his idea of the permanent will of God allowing Himself to become incarnate in His created world. In the *Ambigua* no. 7, Maximus says that the Logos of God and God always and in everything wishes to carry out the mystery of His embodiment,[2] and he emphasizes that the *logoi* reveal the divine purpose. He now combines this idea with that of Evagrius concerning the *logoi* of providence and judgment, but he transforms it in such a way that any connection with the Origenist myth about a pre-historical fall is ruled out. For Maximus, judgment, with its inherent *logos*, which is the principle of an intended differentiation, plays a positive role within the context of providence, the *logos* of which is the principle of

[2]*Patr. Gr.* 91, 1084 CD.

unification without violence to individualized multiplicity. Consequently, creation is to Maximus an act of divine condescension, interpreted in terms of the incarnation of the Logos, introducing a positive element of movement, inherent in beings since their creation, but imprisoned and perverted by sin. In this way creation remains good and related to Christ as the Logos, incarnating Himself. But it is also, at the same time, interpreted within a perspective of fall and sinfulness, and of reconciliation through suffering, a fact that protects us from false optimism. The cosmic Christ is at the same time the Christ of the Cross and of the Resurrection. Only through the Cross and the Resurrection can the world be saved, although it is at all times kept together through its different *logoi* by the Logos Creator. This is indeed the secret of the *logoi* of providence and judgment.

But do these speculations about the *logoi* of creation and their relationship to Christ as the Logos still have relevance today? Or what interpretation of them would help us to a valid comprehension of creation in a Christian perspective today? A kind of parallel to these problems seems to me to be found in the possible relevance of Luther's famous speculation (used in his discussion with Zwingli about the real presence of Christ in the eucharist)about what he called the *ubiquity* (i.e. the all-presence) of Christ everywhere in the created order, a presence due to the fact that Christ's human nature shares the qualities of His divine nature, and yet delivers Him at the same time to the sinner in the eucharistic communion, being really present in the bread and wine. His presence is not a majestic one alone. It is self-delivering, self-emptying, and yet it rests upon the indissoluble relationship between the human and divine nature in Christ, as it was once defined at Chalcedon.

First of all, we might ask what the specific spiritual aim of Maximus was when he developed his thought in this line. As for Luther in his time, it had something to do with a *communion*. Man is lost without constant communion with God, and the road to that saving communion is Christ incarnate. Maximus does not only consider the eucharist in this context. For him several ways of communion are opened up

in Christ as the Logos. Through the contemplation of the
logoi of creation, the soul enters into mystical communion
with the Logos, who gives Himself to it there in virtue of
His primary inhabitation in the *logoi* of created beings. And
this communion has an intermediary value on the way to
mystical communion with God Himself. Through an interior
profound comprehension of the whole of creation via the
principles (*logoi*) of their being, which are also the principles of their future (i.e. of their qualified existence within
the Kingdom of God), the human soul becomes "christian-
ized" and prepares itself for the mystical union with the very
Source and sovereign Principle of all that is.

This communion through the contemplation of the human
mind, i.e. its intelligible faculty, purified through the *vita
practica,* is not of a material character in a gross sense. The
Christian contemplates creation as it were from above, or
from within, and not through its external sensible impressions.
This way of looking at creation may seem to us, living in a
culture marked by empirical research, not only strange but
also standing in contradiction to a modern scientific attitude,
which compels us to start with facts and experiments, and
thus with sensations, although measured and controlled by
modern apparatus. Yet, if we reflect a little more profoundly,
we might ask whether this difference of approach is not of
a rather superficial character. For what is characteristic of a
modern, and truly scientific, view of nature is that we are
dealing not with the materialities of a more ancient kind of
science, but with very minute factors, which are hard to
define without access to the language of symbols and images,
e.g. with the very subtle elements of the atoms, and even
electronic tensions. Even more important, these elements that
form the substance of the "material" world are often only
observable in their effects, and are only describable through
very abstract formulas, or, as we said, through more or less
symbolic images.

Of course, these formulas and symbols reflect as much the
rationality of man comprehending them as the structure of
the world itself. It is thus through the concepts of human
rationality—a rationality that is more than "rational" in a

restricted sense, but must also have access to its speculative power of symbolization—and through them alone that we may get access to a kind of totality of truth about the world in which we live. In addition to that, it remains a fact that it is only through faith in the image of God in man, theologically speaking, that we could also find an indication of the divine intention behind creation and of our being placed within it.

In this situation, with due consideration given to what is characteristic of the way in which we approach creation and nature in our time, it seems to me that Maximus's speculations about the *logoi* come close to us, rather than separating him from us. He might be of help in interpreting this situation in a Christian way, i.e. in its relationship to Christ the Creator and the Consummator. The speculations of a Fr. Pierre Teilhard de Chardin on the evolution of the world toward the *Omega* point also seem to have a certain affinity to those of Maximus. This is the case not least in regard to their common positive evaluation of *movement* as a creative force, although Teilhard, of course, sees things in a more definitely historical and evolutionary perspective.

MAXIMUS AND THE ROLE OF THE UNCREATED ENERGIES IN PALAMISM

This second sub-theme is closely related to the first one. There is obviously a line of development that unites Maximus with Gregory Palamas and the whole Eastern tradition of thinking that emanates from him. In an excellent way John Meyendorff has analyzed the thinking of Gregory, this 14th century Byzantine saint and theological spokesman for the piety of Mount Athos, and also demonstrated its relevance far beyond his own time through his doctrine of the uncreated energies, a doctrine which in many ways parallels the Western Thomist doctrine of the "analogy of being" (*analogia entis*). Now, Maximus in his speculations about the *logoi* of creation establishes himself, in a historical perspective, as a forerunner of Gregory Palamas, since the *logoi* may be interpreted, although Maximus himself did not do so in an explicit way, as energies of God in a Palamite sense.[3]

What can one state with certainty about Maximus's conception of the *logoi* in their double relationship to God (the Logos) and to the concrete world in its manifold manifestations? Are the *logoi* transcendent or immanent, are they created or noncreated? The answer must be a double one. On the one hand Maximus affirms that the *logoi* are pre-existent in God. On the other hand, he also says that God brought them to their realization in concrete creation, according to the general law of the continual presence of God and of the Logos. In a certain way they are, thus, *both transcendent and immanent*. Yet, this immanence does not invite us to conclude that they are created. As immanent they represent, and *are*, the presence of the divine intention and principle of every single nature and species. And as such this intention presents itself as their natural fixity as well as their existential purpose. As realized in the existence of things, they materialize in the created order. Yet they are certainly not themselves created or part of that created order in the sense that they are bound by its material appearance or actual realization.

Are the *logoi* then, in Maximus's thinking, uncreated energies in a more or less Palamite sense? And, further, does this mean that they are as such distinct from the essence of God? The answer—which cannot be a definitive one—should be presented step by step.

The first question indicates the possibility of a certain tension between the absolute unity of the divine Essence and the multiplicity of God's intentions (noncreated). Regarding the *logoi* as such, however, one cannot point to any tension. It is rather a matter of a certain dialectic. It is God who preserves the *logoi* in their unity, but they are nevertheless fixed in Him, such as they are, in Maximus's view. The natural movements of the different species, in conformity with their *logoi* as intentions, designating their purpose in God's total plan, are different according to their differentiation. They

[3]On Gregory Palamas, see John Meyendorff, *St. Gregory Palamas and Orthodox Spirituality*, New York 1974.

converge toward the divine Unity, especially when considered in human contemplation. Thereby, this contemplative activity of man, when properly undertaken in a purified way, reflects the unifying intention of God. In relation to the Logos, the same thing holds true. The Logos *is*, as we have underlined, Himself the many *logoi*, but then the *logoi* may also be said to *be* the one and only Logos, although what we know of them and their variety does not exhaust what is contained in the Logos. Thus there is no complete identity. As differentiated the *logoi* never cease to be different from one another, but their relationship with the Logos is a relationship with their own final principle of unity. At the same time the relation of the Logos to them is in accordance with the principle of His differentiated and incarnational inhabitation in the created world. He encounters us in and through their pluriformity as their unity and ours at the same time.

Maximus uses Biblical images to explain the mystery of the *logoi*, as for instance in the following one. The *logoi* are placed like birds on the branches of the great tree of the Logos, the tree that has grown up from the mustard seed of which the Gospel speaks. Likewise—and now he uses another image—the *logoi* of intelligible beings may be comprehended as the blood of the Logos and the *logoi* of sensible things as the flesh of the Logos, through which manifestations those who are worthy of it may enter into spiritual communion with God.[4] The *logoi* are thus not identical with the essence of God, nor with the empirical forms of existence of the things of the created world.

But this does not necessarily mean that they are divine energies in the sense that Gregory Palamas develops. At this point Fr. Riou has made an important remark. He calls attention to the fact that the Orthodox theologian Vladimir Lossky interpreted the *logoi* in Maximus's theology simply as uncreated energies and that Fr. Sherwood criticized him on this point, accusing him of interpreting Maximus's statements without any real foundation in a Dionysian and Palamite way. But more importantly, Riou also calls attention to a text in

---

[4]See *Gnost* 2, 10; *Patr. Gr.* 90, 1129 A, and *Quaest. ad Thal.* 35; 90, 377 C.

Ambigua no. 22 where Maximus actually uses the expression "energies" about the *logoi*. What that means may, of course, still be discussed (and I think that Maximus's understanding here is influenced first of all by Pseudo-Dionysius), but at least his terminology underlines his very dynamic conception of the *logoi*.[5] I will quote the text without further comment, since it speaks for itself to a great extent.

> In perceiving naturally all the *logoi* that are in the beings, in the infinity of which it contemplates the *energies of God,* the mind, to say the truth, makes numerous and infinite the differences of the divine *energies* it perceives. Indeed, the scientific research of what is really true will have its forces weakened and its procedure embarrassed, if the mind cannot comprehend *how* God is in the *logos* of every special thing and likewise in all the *logoi* according to which all things exist, God who is truly none of the beings and yet truly all the beings and above all the beings. Thus, in a proper sense, all divine energy signifies God properly, *indivisibly and totally via that energy in everything,* whatever the *logos* may be which is capable of conceiving exactly and telling *how* God is it without being divided and without being diversely spread out in the infinite differences of being in which He is as Being . . .[6]

The important thing to notice in these quotations is, of course, the very fact that Maximus feels inclined to term the *logoi* energies. Obviously their nonstatic and dynamic character testifies in itself to the freedom of God's presence in things, being in the whole of creation in its differentiation and yet not being divided, but holding it all together in Himself as Being.

Another great problem remains to be dealt with: is what Maximus wants to express with his *logoi*/energies the

[5]Cf. Riou, *op. cit.,* p. 60.

[6]*Patr. Gr.* 91, 1257 AB; the text is complicated and difficult to interpret, and I rely here on Fr. Riou's own French translation in *op. cit.,* p. 60 f.

same experience and theological concern as that of Gregory Palamas? At this point Fr. Garrigues has expressed himself in a modulated way: the intention of the two writers is the same, he maintains, but their manner of expression is so different that Maximus anticipates the Western doctrine of grace, while Gregory has become the most typical representative of the Eastern tradition.[7] This judgment, however, requires some further comment and correction.

According to Fr. Garrigues there were two possible philosophical approaches to the problem involved: a Platonic and an Aristotelian one. The Platonic attitude—or better, that of Neoplatonism—was inherited by Maximus and Gregory through Pseudo-Dionysius, though one of their common predecessors was also Eunomius who, according to Garrigues, was the pioneer in formulating the basis of a position like that of Gregory Palamas. But Eunomius was an Arian heretic of the fourth century, opposed by the Cappadocian Fathers; he claimed that the very essence of God was accessible to human knowledge. Thus, what Garrigues states does not suggest that Gregory shared the opinion of Eunomius in regard to Trinitarian theology, but that his thinking developed along the same lines. Both want to underline the possibility for man to have access to God Himself, and there is a similarity in their categories. The divine essence in itself cannot be other than pure rest, and thus, according to Gregory, participation in God can only be realized as participation in His energies. But this participation, then, is actually in something other than God, one must conclude, or at least that is Garrigues's contention.

Now Gregory, according to Garrigues, finds himself confronted with a dilemma since he bases himself on the same philosophy as Eunomius: the participation of man in the divine reality must not affect God's very essence, and yet it must be a real participation, through grace, in the divine life. It is for this reason that Gregory makes his decisive distinction in God between His essence and His uncreated energies. But (and this is the point in Garrigues's argument) such a

[7]See J. M. Garrigues, "L'énergie divine et la grâce chez Maxime le Confesseur," *Istina* 19, 1974, pp. 272-296.

distinction threatens the unity of God in order to safeguard His self-sufficiency, or better, His rest in Himself. Gregory's intention is to affirm a real divinization of man, but on his Platonic or Neoplatonic basis he can find no other way out than through his distinction between a fixed Essence and an emanating Energy.

Garrigues finds, however, that there could be another solution to the problem, based on Aristotelian grounds. It is in the simplicity of God rather than in his superessence that one should look for real transcendence. That simplicity is not affected by "the perfect actuality of the divine Being."[8]

As to Maximus, Garrigues argues, he inherited a Platonizing terminology, but through the different stages of his own theological development, particularly his refutation of Origenism and his fight against Monotheletism, he discovered this other possibility (i.e. the Aristotelian approach). Garrigues summarizes this part of his investigation in the following way: "In defining the energy of God as the only power of relationship between the creatures and their Cause, Maximus goes beyond the Neoplatonist concept of processive participation and is in the position to develop a doctrine of participation based on the causality of creative Being in regard to created beings."[9]

But Garrigues does not stop there. He adds a discussion about Maximus's manner of securing the corresponding factor on the part of man, since without a theandric synergism no divinization could be realized. The solution, according to Garrigues, thus is once more an Aristotelian (and Western) one: Maximus professes a *communion of intention*, between God and man, which presupposes an energetic power on the part of God, understood in the way just indicated, and on the part of man a *habitus* of charity given through the causality of divine Grace, impressing itself upon the believer in virtue of the self-emptying (*kenosis*) of Christ.[10]

Here I must take a more critical attitude. I do not think that it is possible to find this specific doctrine of a *habitus* of

[8]*Art. cit.*, p. 281.
[9]*Ibid.*
[10]*Ibid.*, p. 287 f.

grace in Maximus, which Garrigues is looking for, and which would be *supernaturally* impressed upon the believer as the divine charity, even though Maximus does speak explicity about grace and about divine charity operating in man, as well as an impact of Christ upon the Christian. In my opinion, the synergism that Garrigues tries to establish in Maximus is too artificial and too little dialectical, and where then is, the true communion of intention?

I do not pretend to have a final solution to the problem of "energetic communion" in Maximus. Yet, I believe that the Chalcedonian model—here as always—is decisive for him. That is a model in which the Incarnation is not understood in terms of assimiliation (or even assumption) only, but in terms of *reciprocity*. Incarnation is a coming together of the two natures, the divine and the human, a hypostatic (or personal) coming together, that is also a "tropical" one, i.e. a moral and existential coming together, but not a mixture and not an identification of any kind. Even when he speaks about participation (through grace, of course), Maximus preserves the idea of an abyss (between created and uncreated order), but he also speaks of a *"tropical" identity* which renews itself constantly as a divine consolation for man in, and through, the truly human virtues as insights into divine reality. This is precisely what grace means to Maximus, this condescension on the part of God that lets itself be continually grasped and "materialized" in human insights and human virtues. It is as authentic reflections of their archetype that these insights and virtues are divine, but not in an ontological sense. However, in the same measure as one might comprehend what they reflect, this comprehension is rather a participation in the condescending divine energies than in the impenetrable essence of God. The law of God's continual presence is not a law of assimilation or assumption, but of theandric and salvific dialectic.

This (personal) conclusion brings us finally to the question of Maximus's eschatology (i.e. his understanding of the end of history and the fulfillment of all things).

ESCHATOLOGY AND MYSTICAL UNION

In the earlier modern studies on Maximus's theology—those of von Balthasar, Hausherr, Sherwood, I.-H. Dalmais (an excellent Dominican Maximian scholar whose articles, translation, and commentaries are spread over a number of magazines and other publications), Völker, and myself—very little is said about the eschatology of Maximus. In more recent studies—particularly those of Fr. Riou and of Fr. Garrigues—the term "eschatological" is found in many places. Thus, it seems important to put the question: why this difference? The answer is certainly not that it is only recently that a traditional eschatological theology has been discovered in Maximus, which nobody had noticed before. The reason is rather that the more recent authors have had the intention of underlining the eschatological dimension as one more of the dimensions that are relevant within the Maximian theological universe.

But what do we mean by this dimension? And what are the specific values of this (additional) perspective, particularly in view of our own time? This is the problem that will be discussed in this final section of this chapter.

Let me propose, immediately, the following opinion. Eschatology, as a separate subject in a later traditional sense, plays a very restricted role in the theology of Maximus. Yet, *eschatology as a dimension of theology* is very important, if it is understood as a permanent dimension of transcendence opening up everlasting perspectives. In his vision of Christian life Maximus does not know of an absolute break between existence *hic et nunc* and life after death.

There exists, beyond doubt, a difference of fullness, but not a break, and there is no question of a completely new creation, which would not have its starting point already here and now. Almost no aspect of spiritual life is found entirely on one or the other side of the iron curtain of corporal death. Thus, the eschatological dimension is almost identical with Maximus's theology of divinization and with his mystical theology, properly speaking.

I propose, therefore, just a few compressed considerations of this basic theme, representing a kind of summary and conclusion of Maximus's theology as a totality.

Maximus's attitude in regard to different theories of man's *mystical ecstasy* is very important in this context, for it shows the authentic character of his eschatology. Among his predecessors we may recognize *three types of speculation about ecstasy.* One of them is the Evagrian type of *emigration,* according to which the final aim of human life is a naked intellect receiving the knowledge of the Divine Trinity. Another is the concept of a continual "emigration," in the category of *epectasis,* characteristic of a Gregory of Nyssa, where the soul loses itself in "sober drunkenness" in God. Finally, there is the concept of ecstasy that we find in Pseudo-Dionysius, where the soul is outside of itself due to a passive *suffering* of the divine reality, a particular but also an everlasting experience.

Now, we may conclude that the first type of ecstasy takes place within, and not outside of, the natural capacity of human intelligence. The second one indicates an emigration outside of oneself and of everything, and thus it never finds its final rest, but continues to move into God forever. According to the third conception, it seems as if the soul nevertheless receives a kind of information of an intellectual character about Divinity itself. What can be said of Maximus's position is that he is critical of all of these types of ecstatic theology, although he has learned much from them all.

In regard to the Evagrian type, he seems to be more radical. He states more forcefully that in mystical union the intellect becomes unconscious of itself, and that it refuses to accept in the natural capacity of its soul knowledge of the Trinitarian reality. In regard to the Gregorian concept of *epectasis* Maximus is sceptical of its philosophical consequences; he cannot identify eternal rest with a movement, since this implies a relativization of both rest and movement. Yet, he is quite sympathetic toward the Gregorian paradox of divine presence and human distance at the same time. He himself uses an expression like "movement of the always fixed" in dialectical interchange with his own precise defini-

tion of mystical union as "rest of continual movement."
Finally, in regard to the Ps.-Dionysian concept of ecstasy,
Maximus modifies the idea of "suffering the Divine" in the
sense that the latter only implies the idea of "suffering to
be moved," and he adds that he who loves something "suffers
ecstasy" vis-à-vis this phenomenon as loved.

To Maximus, as a matter of fact, mystical ecstasy implies
a real departure from oneself in order to enter into the ineffable sphere of the Divinity as in the case of Ps. Dionysius
the Areopagite, since this radical emigration is not brought
to its realization except through the grace of God. Yet, this
does not mean that the human effort simply disappears. On
the contrary, he speaks also of a *"gnomic emigration"* toward
that which alone, and finally, may satisfy his demand (i.e.
the natural desire of man), and thus bring his entire movement to its rest, to God Himself.

Consequently, we have two equally important factors in
regard to mystical union: "the voluntary emigration" on the
part of man and the illuminating grace of God. Once more
we can see that Chalcedonian theology serves as the model
of interpretation for Maximus. Unification takes place without confusion and change, whether it be of the created nature
or the uncreated nature, bringing them nevertheless into an
inseparable unity.

This last observation is of the same importance for his
theolgy of deification. In *Ambigua 10,* Maximus says that
God

> makes Himself human for the sake of man through
> His philanthropy, in the same measure as man, forti-
> fied by charity, divinizes himself for God; man is
> enraptured by God in mind to the unknowable, so far
> as man has manifested, through virtues, the God by
> nature invisible.[11]

Here we find demonstrated that reciprocity between God and
man which remains the basis of all Maximian theology. For
here there is a correspondence between the ecstasy of man

[11]*Patr. Gr.* 91, 1113 BC.

toward God and the manifestation, in him, of his proper nature in virtues. This manifestation is conceived as a kind of incarnation or embodiment of the Logos, and these virtues are seen as reflections of the divine attributes. As such they are manifestations of the ecstasy of God toward man—to use Ps.-Dionysian terminology—and therefore they represent, beyond any doubt, the "encouragement" that is promised to man in mystical union. The natural desire of man in search for God, thus, finds its rest in Him through a process of interpenetration, which preserves both the gulf between the natures and the fixity of the divine and human, but communicates—simultaneously—the modes of existence both as human virtues and as divine attributes.

This is, then, the eschatological dimension of Maximus's theology. It is certainly quite "existential" and "modern" in many ways. But does it also have something to say to us about our own eschatological questions, properly speaking? The speculation of a Pierre Teilhard de Chardin and of the modern so-called "theology of hope" (J. Moltmann on the Protestant side and J. B. Metz on the Roman Catholic) have taught us that absolute reality (i.e. the reality of the cosmic Christ) does not necessarily have to be above us, but could also be understood as being before us. But, we must ask, is that particular (and very modern) perspective entirely absent from Maximus's theology? I do not believe so. The movement of final ecstasy about which he is speaking directs itself toward a final goal, and this goal is both here and beyond ourselves; precisely as a goal it always appears to our desire to go beyond ourselves in order to find, in God, the rest that is the absolute consummation of human life. This perspective is definitely universal, i.e. (in this context) not limited to cosmological and nonchronological levels.

And what is even more important for Maximus, yes, of quite capital importance for him, is this "consolation" or "encouragement" that through the vision that we achieve for ourselves through our practical efforts and our actual experiences assures us that we are on the right way, although we have not yet reached the final goal. This "consolation" always awakens our natural aspirations, without letting us believe, at any moment, that this final goal and union with God will be a fruit of our efforts in themselves.

Deification or divinization is the final goal of man. Greater it could not be. And yet it is always a reminder of the fact of the Incarnation, because man's divinization remains a consequence of God's "humanization" in the incarnation of the Logos. Thus, in Maximus's theology, christological and anthropological convictions go together in complete harmony, and the basis of this is in his concept of reciprocity. Therefore, the incarnational presence of Christ is decisive at every point in his theological system. Every dimension of it is in a sense a christological dimension. In the Appendix, we shall deal with this fact in terms of Christ's eucharistic presence, and the problem of symbolic nearness and concretion that this implies.

Symbol and Mystery in St Maximus

With particular reference to the doctrine of
the eucharistic presence

In this additional chapter we shall illustrate a special aspect of what has been treated more systematically above. Its background is a contribution to the first scholarly symposium on St. Maximus which was held at Fribourg, Switzerland, in September 1980. This contribution will make more concrete the originality of Maximus the Confessor.

The precise problem at stake is this: *To what extent is Maximus's conception of the eucharist a realistic or a purely symbolist one?* In trying to answer this question I propose that Maximus's understanding of the key terms *mysterion* and *symbolon* should be considered more closely.

The problem treated in this appendix has become more acutely relevant to me in recent years. Being myself involved in the present ecumenical dialogue between Roman Catholics and Lutherans, I have realized the importance of the basic agreement that exists today between Lutherans and Roman Catholics on *the real presence of the very body and blood of our Lord Jesus Christ in the eucharist,* and on the mode of that presence as directly linked to the elements of bread and wine, and also the agreement on the fact that this realistic understanding is of basic importance for our notion of what happens in the communion of the believers. We may disagree on the way in which this presence comes about, and also on the role and function of the faith of the believers in regard to their communion and the efficacy of the Sacrament. On *what* is communicated there is, however, a consensus.[1]

Historically there had existed far more of a disagreement between Lutherans and Reformed. Since the Leuenberg Agreement of 1973 between these two positions, a considerable amount of *rapprochement* has been reached, precisely because it has been possible to agree on a more realistic understanding of the real presence. Now, both Roman Catholics and Lutherans are in an initial phase of dialogue with the Orthodox, and it is thus of great importance to know more exactly where the positions are in Eastern and Western tradition in regard to the understanding of the Real Presence. The issue of realistic versus symbolistic understanding is certainly differently conceived between Eastern and Latin traditions than between, say, Lutheran and Reformed traditions, but there are certainly some similarities between the symbolistic traditions nevertheless. It seems to be particularly relevant in precisely this situation to analyze the position of such a great figure of the East as St. Maximus the Confessor.

Besides this modern ecumenical impetus, however, there are also some considerations of a more historical character that have impelled me to analyze this problem as an essential part of Maximus's theology. Dr. Anna Marie Aagaard—who for many years has been working on the theology of a much later representative of the Eastern Christian tradition, St. Symeon the New Theologian—called my attention to the fact that Fr. John Meyendorff in his *Byzantine Theology* states that the symbolistic understanding of the eucharist which is characteristic of Pseudo-Dionysius the Areopagite (and on which Maximus is basically dependent) became a problem to the Eastern Church in the eighth century, when the defenders of the images, such as Theodore the Studite, had to reject it. But Fr. Meyendorff also states that Symeon the New Theologian in this respect represents a "realistic sacramental-

[1]We have expressed the degree of this consensus in the document of the official Catholic/Lutheran Commission, called *The Eucharist*, Geneva 1980.

ism."[2] Since she herself doubted the last statement, she felt that the whole problem had to be reconsidered. The similarities and differences between the Areopagite and Maximus are obviously part of such a revision. Thus I was prompted to deal with this problem anew within the context of Maximus's theology.

BASIC ASPECTS OF THE PROBLEM

All Maximus scholars know that there is a basic problem in regard to Maximus's understanding of the eucharist proper on account of the scarcity of source texts. Although some scholars have regarded it possible to construct a Maximian eucharistic doctrine (either with a negative or with a positive result from the traditional point of view), it remains a fact that (in the words of Walther Völker) "Maximus never expressed himself succinctly about the Eucharist," but "restricted himself to rare, not always transparent, remarks which offer almost insurmountable difficulties because of their sweeping allegorical character and their fragmentary concentration."[3]

Against this fact it is rather strange that Polycarp Sherwood (a very accurate student of Maximus) is able to recognize no less than twelve texts dealing with the eucharist, of which six are supposed to deal with the problem of communion. For my own part, I have not been able to find more than four passages (possibly five) that deal with the eucharist proper in its communion aspect, and they are all of such a character that a succinct "doctrine of the eucharist" cannot be constructed on their basis.[4]

Thus, the source basis for our discussion is rather meager. Nevertheless, I will propose later an analysis of these texts, which may indicate some basic Maximian understanding of

---

[2]See Meyendorff, *op. cit.,* p. 203, cf. p. 75.
[3]See Völker, *op. cit.,* p. 472.
[4]They are: *Quaest. dub.* 41; *Patr. Gr.* 90, 820 A; *Myst.* 21; *Patr. Gr.* 91, 696 D-697A; 24; 704 D-705 A; *Epilogue* 709 C, and possibly, *Or. Dom.*; *Patr. Gr.* 90, 877 C.

the eucharist (and one not necessarily identical with that of the Areopagite).

Another basic problem is that Maximus in his *Mystagogia* (which is supposed to be his commentary on the Liturgy of the Holy Eucharist) leaves out a direct commentary on the *Anaphora* itself. He indicates a reason for this, in that he refers to the interpretation of the Areopagite in the latter's *De ecclesiastica hierarchia*, which he does not want to repeat or compete with (although he actually does comment on things that the Areopagite also treats at length). Several scholars have not felt content with this explanation; they have rather referred to a *discipline of silence* (relevant both to the eucharist itself and particularly to Maximus as a lay monk) as the reason for his reluctance. This is the case of, for example, Alain Riou, while Hans Urs von Balthasar is resistant about it and René Bornert discusses this possibility more openly. As a matter of fact, such reluctance on behalf of a layman may also be supported by the position of the Areopagite.[5]

Whatever the reason may be, it is a fact that we have no explicit indication of how Maximus interprets the Holy Communion, or how he looks upon the eucharistic presence. Of course, one may argue that precisions at this point were not yet necessary, and that therefore Maximus's situation was much freer than that of the eighth century. On the other hand, problems immanent in the theology of Maximus itself should indicate a necessary position-taking. For my own part, I think that Maximus has taken a position already, and that, although he may not be explicit about it, he indicates it in his very attitude to eucharistic communion. His actual *discipline of silence* points, at least, to a respect for this moment of the liturgy (from consecration to communion), which singles it out as being of another value and significance than all the other symbolic acts of the liturgy. But we shall return to that suggestion later, after having analyzed more in detail the few texts that we have.

[5]See A. Riou, *op. cit.,* p. 165, n. 37; von Balthasar, *op. cit.,* p. 365; and not least R. Bornert, *Les Commentaires Byzantins de la Divine Liturgie du VIIe au XVe siècle,* Paris 1966, p. 105f.

Two things have certainly favored those who rank Maximus among those of the "symbolistic" school of interpretation: (a) his reference to the Areopagite as an authoritative interpreter of the mystery of the eucharist; and (b) his own symbolistic interpretation of the parts of the liturgy that he comments upon. However, for a more precise understanding, we are bound to discuss both what the influence of the Areopagite really implies and the exact interpretation of the few passages where Maximus actually deals with the eucharistic presence and the character and implications of the communion. And it is quite clear—also from the delicate way in which Maximus both uses and modifies the work of his predecessors in other aspects of his theology—that only a minute analysis of what Maximus actually says will give sufficient evidence of his own exact position. As far as the eucharist is concerned, this work has not yet been done. What I propose here, therefore, is only a beginning.

Some of the frames of reference for such an analysis, however, are obvious. One of these frames of reference is of course Maximus's theology of the Incarnation of the Logos. Another, linked to it through his understanding of the Incarnation as being threefold, is his idea of the three laws and the synthesis that they imply, since Christ incarnate holds it all together. Incarnation, understood in the terms of the Council of Chalcedon, implies for man an access to divinity through the modes of this incarnation. Therefore, the world, the Scriptures, and the Church together and in mutual relationship may be interpreted in anthropological terms, according to the *Mystagogia*. The whole world is subsumed under the Logos as differentiated in the *logoi* of things. All of Scripture is subsumed under the Logos as differentiated in the *logoi* of the divine economy. The whole of mankind, though differentiated socially and ontologically, and together with the rest of creation separated from the divine world, is subsumed under Christ as its head, who leads it on the way to perfection and deification.

Consequently, Maximus's understanding of the cosmos, since the liturgy necessarily takes place within the context of the cosmos, is of importance to our problem. More par-

ticularly, his understanding of Scripture and of the interpretation of Scripture is vital. There the function of images,
types, and symbols and their relationship to salvation are at
stake in a way that has to be parallel to that of the liturgy and
the function of the sacraments. This parallelism, however,
must be worked out precisely.

Finally, there is the frame of reference that is represented
by Maximus's understanding of spiritual development. To
which stage of this development is the eucharist and particularly eucharistic communion to be related? In other words,
is the bodily eating and drinking an expression of the earlier
and lower stages of the process of spiritual perfection or
do they pertain to all or even to the last stage, and to what
extent has communion even to do with deification?

Within these contexts or frames of reference in Maximus's
theology, we can easily see a number of questions appear in
regard to the problem of eucharistic presence and the importance of the oral communion of the believers. Let me mention
some of them, and at the same time indicate the basic structure of my presentation.

1. We started with a somewhat crude distinction
between a "symbolistic" and a "realistic" understanding of the eucharist. A preliminary question, then,
would be *how Maximus's position has been judged by
scholars until now.*

2. A second preliminary question, since Maximus
obviously refers to and depends on *Pseudo-Dionysius
the Areopagite,* is *how* the position of the latter in
regard to our distinction *is to be evaluated.*

3. A third question relates to Maximus's *understanding of Scripture,* seen in the perspective of his
view of the Incarnation and in regard to the possible
parallelism between man's access to the Logos through
Scriptural revelation and his access to him through
the eucharist. Since incarnational language is equally
valid in relation to Scripture as in relation to the
eucharist, and since a purely symbolistic interpretation

of the latter seems to imply that the eucharistic symbols are equivalent to the symbolistic language of Scripture, this opens the question, to what extent can similar distinctions be made in regard to different parts of Scripture as should be expected within the liturgy, e.g. between rites that come before the consecration on the one hand and the eucharistic sacrifice (as far as that is presupposed) and the eucharistic communion on the other. Maximus's general use of the terms *mysterion* and *symbolon* must be observed at this point.

4. A fourth question is closely related to this: is there a difference in Maximus between what we might call *"gnostic" communion* with the *Logos* through the interpretation of Scripture, and the *sacramental communion* with Christ? And what is the implication of *experience* in this context?

5. We cannot come to a proper view of Maximus's understanding of eucharistic communion unless we analyze *the four texts,* where he explicitly deals with it. Therefore, I suggest that such an analysis be made with a particular stress on the *terminology* used. Here again we must observe the terms *mysterion* and *symbolon,* but certainly not only them.

6. In addition to this, we should notice another problem. In regard to communion with the Logos through Scripture, Maximus underlines (as a successor of the Alexandrian tradition, etc.) the *analogy* that exists between what is received and the preparedness of the receiver. For a symbolistic understanding of the eucharist, this idea—the idea of what is usually called the "worthiness"—may be equally applicable to the eucharist. For a realistic understanding, however, again a distinction must be introduced, namely, between the full presence of Christ in the sacrament, on the one hand, and the personal receptivity of the communicant, on the other. Linked to this is the question how *the terminology of eucharistic transformation* is used by

Maximus. Is the aspect of sacramental efficacy or the
aspect of receptivity predominant?

"SYMBOLIST" OR "REALIST" IN THE
VIEW OF THE SCHOLARS

At the outset, two extreme positions seem to be represented. On the one hand, an old scholar like G. E. Steitz
considers Maximus a clear representative of what he calls
"the Alexandrian symbolism," even as "the most fragrant
blossom of all Alexandrinism."[6] On the other side W.
Lampen recognizes the traditional eucharistic doctrine in Maximus,
though without an appropriate analysis.[7] The judgments of
more recent scholars have been more carefully phrased. Sherwood tends to side with Lampen, in the sense that he both
finds Maximus relatively explicit and states that we are permitted to say that for Maximus "the eucharist is at the heart
of the Christian life,"[8] a conclusion that Völker finds "not
exactly surprising."[9] Von Balthasar, on the other hand, seems
to side with Steitz, since he says that the conclusion of the
latter is "certainly right."[10] Later, in a discussion of Maximus's silence about the matter, he says that one must presume
that Maximus was not in a position to regard what Christ
had instituted as "pure reality" as being only a symbolic
phenomenon.[11] Völker regards the oscillating position of the
scholars as due to the meagerness of the textual witnesses,
and refrains from a definite position.[12]

A well worked out position I have only found in Bornert
distinguishing first of all between two groups of texts, one
indicating the "symbolic" character of the eucharist and one

[6]See G. E. Steitz, "Die Abendmahlslehre des Maximus Confessor,"
Jahrbuch für deutsche Theologie 11, 1886, p. 238.
[7]See W. Lampen, "De Eucharistie-leer van S. Maximus Confessor,"
Studia Catholica 2, 1926, pp. 35-54.
[8]See *St. Maximus the Confessor, The Ascetic Life* . . . , p. 79 ff.
[9]See Völker, *op. cit.*, p. 472, n. 2.
[10]Von Balthasar, *op. cit.*, p. 316.
[11]*Ibid.*, p. 364 f.
[12]*Op. cit.*, p. 472, n. 2.

which presents the eucharist as the sacrament of union with God and deification. Based on the latter, and referring also to Maximus's more explicit statements about baptism, Bornert feels entitled to conclude that Maximus's development of eucharistic symbolism is not anti-realist. Realism and symbolism are mutually related. However, Bornert also underlines that Maximus does not make the important distinction between "efficacious sacramental symbolism" and "a purely representative liturgical symbolism," where the former "realizes that which it signifies," while the latter is "a simple aid to contemplation."[13] However helpful these precisions are, I should like to add already here that the qualifications "purely" and "simple" seem to me to go beyond what Maximus would actually agree to. It is not only a lack of distinction on his part, but perhaps a somewhat different view of the problem which prevents him from making that kind of precise distinction.

THE POSITION OF THE AREOPAGITE

Since the source material that explicitly expresses Maximus's understanding of the eucharist is so limited, his admitted dependence on the Areopagite necessarily attracts more attention. But could his views supposedly coincide with those of the latter? Detailed analyses by von Balthasar (especially in his study of the *Gnostic Centuries*) and by Völker (in regard to spiritual development) and others, have shown a considerable but qualified dependence on Pseudo-Dionysius in general. However, one should not conclude from Maximus's reference to Ps. Dionysius in the *Mystagogia* that he has no opinion of his own. As to the lack of an explication of the Anaphora, the reason cannot possibly be simply the one that this had been treated by the Areopagite already, since he does comment on other moments of liturgy in spite of the fact that Ps. Dionysius had already done so.

However, his reference to Ps. Dionysius must be taken seriously. It is only if differences can be demonstrated that

[13]Bornert, *op. cit.*, p. 117 f.

we can conclude that Maximus's opinion on the communion, for example, is different from that of Ps. Dionysius.

But how then shall we characterize the Areopagite's own understanding of the eucharist? Any superficial glance at what he says in his *Ecclesiastical Hierarchy* about the eucharist will confirm the suspicion that here the perspective is almost totally "symbolistic." This, however, is not in a superficial sense. The purpose of the eucharist is unification by illumination, but its instrumentality is basically of a demonstrative character. Thus all the parts of the liturgy have in essence the same function, although there may be differences of degree. It is the Church as an illuminating agent that performs the eucharist within its own community and vis-à-vis the individual believer. The communion represents a culmination, but the participation in the body and blood of Jesus Christ as such seems to have little or no particular relevance. Bornert summarizes correctly that to the Areopagite the eucharist is above all a (illuminating) means of union with God the One.[14]

In regard to the moment of communion, certain elements are particularly notable. First of all, the Anaphora itself is called *symbolikè hierurgia* and this is precisely the perspective which dominates. The whole act is seen, as it were, from above. It is the way in which the hierarch acts that is significant, not the particular presence of Christ, nor the actualization of his sacrifice, nor the communion as reception of him. The *Anamnesis* referred to seems to be of the Last Supper of Jesus, and the model character of that meal is shown in the way the gifts are distributed. The point of view is certainly that of the Incarnation. But the Incarnation is seen as an act through which the one and single divine nature of the Logos enters the complex and manifold sphere of the world. Therefore, *the symbolism of the communion lies in the fact that the gifts are multiplied.* Ps. Dionysius himself says this explicitly: symbolically the hierarch multiplies the unity and thereby performs the most holy service. This certainly indicates the coming to us of the Lord, but its function is primarily demonstrative, and only secondarily the communicating of a sacramental reality.[15]

One could, of course, insist that such illumination for Ps. Dionysius *is* sacramental, and correctly so, but this does not eliminate the fact that it is not the content of the eucharistic gifts that is of main importance to him but rather *the demonstrative quality of their distribution*. On the part of the communicants, what is added is mostly a moral appeal, implied, of course, in the fact that through the distribution the communicants are united among themselves. One is, therefore, inclined to agree with René Rocques, an outstanding expert on Ps. Dionysius, when he underlines that nothing reminds us of the body and blood of Christ, and that the eucharistic communion for Ps. Dionysius more relates us to God in His unity (though Trinitarian, of course) than to participation in Christ's humanity.[16] But if this is the basic view of the Areopagite, we may at least ask ourselves when we come to Maximus's own texts how far he shares this view.

"COMMUNION" THROUGH THE SCRIPTURES

It is Maximus's conviction that the Logos always and in all "wants to effect the mystery of His embodiment." Both the Origenist myth and the Dionysian vision were influential to the way in which he conceived this constant process of incarnation, but his final and total understanding of it is certainly his own. Things belong together in Maximus's theological universe. The key to it is the doctrine of incarnation, the binding formula of which is that of the Council of Chalcedon. It is the Logos becoming man in Jesus Christ (the third and final incarnation) that is the model and paradigm of the whole process of incarnation. This process is certainly interpreted in that perspective and from that starting point. This fact, however, does not exclude a high degree of parallelism between the three basic incarnations: in the *logoi* of

---

[15]See *De hier. eccles.* 12; *Patr. Gr.* 3, 444 **AB**.

[16]See R. Rocques, *L'univers Dionysien. Structure hiérarchique du monde selon le Pseudo-Denys,* Paris 1954, p. 268 f.

things, the *logoi* of Scripture, and the *logos* in man. The Origenist-Evagrian double concept of providence and judgment, reinterpreted and stripped of heresies inherent in the Origenist myth, helped Maximus to demonstrate how the structure of the cosmos and the economy of salvation belong together within a basically anthropo-cosmical perspective of christological dignity. This total system now contains an important element of movement. Cosmologically this may be characterized through the double concept of *expansion* and *concentration*. Christologically it is expressed through an equivalent vision of the "becoming thick" and "becoming thin," which corresponds to Christ's coming into the world and his return to the Father (though from then on also as man as representative of all believers and mankind). In *Amb. 33*, this is most clearly linked to the idea of the threefold "incarnation," and also to the three general laws of the world: the natural law, the written law, and the law of grace.[17]

This shows clearly how incarnational terminology could naturally be used about Scripture. In all three cases the principle of embodiment is the same, although there is a difference of degree and, as it were, historical culmination. This lack of difference in essence on the one hand and difference of degree and development in an economic perspective on the other now seems logically to lead to certain consequences for Maximus's understanding of the sacraments, particularly of the eucharist. For on the one hand, there can be a perfect parallelism of terminology in the description of both. On the other hand, there should be a difference of intensity. Let us very briefly illustrate this.

First of all, we have statements by Maximus where communion terminology is actually used in regard to the first two types of incarnation, and—by implication—not least to Scripture. I refer again to *Quaest. ad Thal.* 35, where the question is about the eating of the flesh and blood of the Logos without crushing his bones. Here Maximus says that when the Logos wanted to come into being, he put down into the world the natural *logoi* of the "conceptions" of his divin-

[17]*Patr. Gr.* 91, 1285 C-1288 A.

ity. The distinction was then that the *logoi* of intelligible things should serve as his blood and the *logoi* of sensible things as his flesh. His unbroken bones, however, are *logoi* that concern the insight into divinity. To eat his flesh, then, is to know the visible things, and to drink his blood is to know the intelligible things.[18] In this eating, of course, the relationship to scriptural revelation is also implied, even more so since later in the alternative interpretations of *Quaest. ad Thal.* 35 the whole process of spiritual development is involved. Thus flesh is interpreted as virtue, blood as knowledge (through *theoria*) and bones as the mystical union (*theologia*). Flesh and blood are also seen as the *logoi* of judgment and providence (i.e. *oikonomia*), while the bones are the hidden *logoi* of divinity.

Another reference to communion terminology is found in *Quaest. ad Thal.* 36, although only indirectly, since the question deals with the law of the Israelites to eat the flesh but not to consume the blood of slaughtered animals. Here it is said, among other things, that Christ as sacrifice is different, for he gives blood together with the flesh. This is said to refer to the relationship between the inner sense of the commandments (in Scripture) and the outward realization of them in *praxis*. Drinking the blood is to take the commandments into the mind, and eating the flesh is to put them into practice.[19] We have here at the same time an indirect reference to the motif of becoming "thick" and "thin": Through the praxis of virtue the Logos becomes "thick." Through the understanding of the commandments, he becomes, as it were, "thinner," more spiritual (although virtue and understanding in themselves are equally important).

This now leads to a number of texts where this incarnation/elevation dynamism is directly related to the way in which man deals with Scripture. In *Quaestiones et Dubia* 61, it is most clearly expressed: The Logos that is hidden in the ten commandments "takes body" in us, going down with us through *praxis* and bringing us upward again through *gnosis*, elevating us until we reach the highest of all the command-

[18]Ed. Laga-Steel, p. 239.
[19]Ed. Laga-Steel, p. 243.

ments, that which says: "The Lord, thy God, the Lord is one." A number of texts from the *Gnostic Centuries* could also be quoted.[20] This pertains to the basic difference between a literal reading of Holy Scriptures and a spiritual/anagogical understanding of them. Völker and others have presented us with good summaries. For our own purpose it may be sufficient to refer precisely to the *Mystagogia*, Chapter 6, which depicts Scripture as a man and does it as a clear parallel to the church building, where the liturgy is celebrated. There we learn that both man and Scripture can be said to consist of body, soul, mind, and spirit. The body is understood both as the Old Testament (while the New Testament is the rest) and also in the whole of Scripture as that which is letter in a historical sense, while the meaning and scope of what is written is soul. One may also distinguish between letter as the body and the hidden truth as spirit. This shows clearly again the anthropological/christological perspective of Maximus's vision: When the Logos becomes incarnate in the Scriptures, he becomes, as it were, already a man. Thus his continued life as man on earth in the Church is a parallel to this presence in Scripture (where, I think, the stones of the building are like the letters, and what these stones contain is like the meaning and mind and spirit of scriptural revelation).

In regard to Maximus's parallelism here and to his understanding of Scripture, there are, however, two more details that we need to observe. One is the function of the terminology of *symbol* and *mystery*, the other is the question whether in Scripture there are clear indications of differences of degree.

As to *symbol* and *mystery* we must be very brief. "Symbol" for Maximus does not have a special position. In most cases it may be replaced by other terms like "type" or "icon." Yet, the term "type" is more often linked to people and used in the perspective of the economy of salvation. "Type" also has a fixed counterpart: the *archetype*. Other synonyms are also relevant, e.g. "shadow" (*skiá*) and "riddle" (*ainigma*) with their counterpart, "truth" (*aletheia*), and in a more general sense "plurality" with its counterpart "simplicity," which, as

[20]See II, 37; *Patr. Gr.* 90, 1141 C; 41, 1144 AB; 47, 1145 B; 58, 1149 B; 59, 1149 C; 60, 1149 CD.

Völker[21] points out, is a sign that Maximus adopts the Dionysian perspective of the world. A special problem is represented by the term *"icon,"* and this leads us on to the question of differences of degree. Bornert—who most helpfully tried to work out the parallelism of terminology and interpretation between Scripture and liturgy in Maximus in relation to the problem of symbolism—claims to have established a decisive difference between "icon" and "type" in Maximus's understanding of Scripture. "Types" are mostly found in the Old Testament, while the Gospel contains the "icon" of the true things (*symbolon* here being more an equivalent to "type"). In Maximus's interpretations of the rites of liturgy, however, "symbol" takes the place of "icon." There it is the symbol that contains the mysteries of our salvation. Bornert presupposes that this shift is due to the influence of Ps. Dionysius. This contention may seem a little formalistic, but some of its implications must be discussed. We shall return later to the question of differences of degree.[22]

What particularly interests us here, however, is the relationship between *symbol* (with its synonyms) and *mystery*. The symbol is always to Maximus a vessel in which a truth is hidden (and it can as such be seen as an expression of the salvific incarnation of the Logos), a vessel the function of which is to become transparent to its content. The same truth remains nevertheless a "mystery." It is its character of *mysterion* (a divine truth that is not naturally available to man) that necessitates its symbolic representation. In order that this mystery be communicated, it must be revealed. It is not enough that the Logos is hidden in the mysterious *logoi* of Scripture: the Logos Himself must actively work for their revelation. This happens through the economy of salvation. Therefore, there is a difference of degree both between the second and the third of the three incarnations and between the Old Testament and the Gospel. In *Cap. Theol.* II, 46, Maximus expresses most wonderfully the activity of Christ as the link between the symbols and their mystery. Just as the Apostles out of fear for the Jews sat behind doors shut after the death of Christ, but received the risen Lord in their midst, so is the Logos secretly active behind the doors of the senses, greeting them with the kiss of peace which is *apátheia,* breathing His spirit upon them and showing them "the symbols of His own mysteries."[23]

Christ thus must Himself open up the secrets of Scripture and its symbols. They are symbols of His mysteries, and the link between them is made effective only by the spiritual activity of the Lord Himself. It is the historical Incarnation and its fulfillment in Christ's glorification (and then also in the activities of the Spirit in the Church) that makes the content and reality of the symbols alive. For this reason Maximus also underlines that Christ is his own "type" or his own forerunner.

This leads to some basic considerations of Maximus's use of the term *mysterion.* It is a very widely used term indeed[24] but there is, nevertheless, a basic sense of this word that is decisive for all the ways it is used. Maximus indicates this in several places. In *Quaest. ad Thal.* 61, he calls the incarnation in man (the third incarnation) "the great mystery." In *Quaest. ad Thal.* 60, he describes the "mystery of Christ" in a most central text and in the Chalcedonian terms of hypostatic union. *Quaest. ad Thal.* 64, again a central text, depicts the whole of Christianity as "the new mystery." The Incarnation is the center of this great mystery, and therefore we may also (with Maximus) talk of *"the whole of the mystery of the divine economy"* and regard this, including its implications for the Church, as the very center of Maximus's understanding of mystery, pertaining both to Scripture and liturgy.

Thus, *symbol and mystery belong together.* It is Christ the Lord Himself, who through His historical Incarnation and glorification and His further acts in the Church and the believers establishes the living link between them and the salvific effects that they serve as part of the divine economy, the summary of all mysteries.

But what then about the difference of degree, in Scripture and elsewhere? If there is, according to Maximus, an eco-

---

[23]*Patr. Gr.* 90, 1145 B; cf. *Amb.* 10; 91, 1132 D.
[24]See Völker, *op. cit.,* p. 283, n. 5.

nomically/historically based difference of degree, then this will affect the parallelism of the symbolism in Scripture and in the liturgy. As a matter of fact, it is not only logical that the difference between the preliminary "type" and the fulfilling "icon," which Bornert claimed to have discovered in Maximus's scriptural understanding, should have a counterpart in his interpretation of the liturgy, but precisely that the Gospel proper (and particularly the words spoken by Jesus Himself, before and after His resurrection) should have a counterpart of quality in the *epikletic* presence and the communion of the eucharist. I do not pretend to be able to prove this perfect parallelism in regard to the degrees of difference, but let us at least look at what is said about the difference in relation to Scripture, including some of the attached problems indicated earlier, and then go on to a more rigorous analysis of the communion texts proper.

What Maximus distinguishes qualitatively within Scripture was already indicated in connection with the suggestions of Bornert. But let us see how it is done. Maximus certainly makes the traditional distinctions between "literal" (*katà grammata*) interpretations and those according to the deeper sense (*katà theorian*). He also distinguishes between different kinds of "letters," and between our relationship to these "letters" before and after the Incarnation. The Old Testament is usually considered equal with the Law, and Maximus emphasizes that God became man in order to fulfill the Law spiritually, and thereby to destroy the dominance of "the letters."[25] On the background of this, the prophets of the Old Testament are of a higher significance than the Law itself.[26]

There is thus a basic difference between the Old and New Testaments (and the quality of the prophets depends on their pointing to the truth of the New Testament revelation), but this does not prevent Maximus from regarding the grace of the New Dispensation as being mystically contained already in the Old. Neither is the Law as such disposed of. Even if it is "becoming old" through the letters, it is renewed through

[25]See *Quaest. ad Thal.* 50; ed. Laga-Steel, p. 381.
[26]See *ibid.* 63; *Patr. Gr.* 90, 677 B.

grace.[27] It is thus impossible to absolutize the difference (obviously, primarily because the *logoi* of the commandments already contain the Logos). It remains a fact that the Law is only a shadow of the Gospel, while the latter is the very image (*icon*) of the good things to come.[28] Therefore, the shining clothes of the scene of the Transfiguration represent the manifestations of the Gospels (which are "more thin").[29]

What is striking here is that it is "the Gospels" and "the Gospel" that are singled out, not the New Testament as such. Is it not an indication that the bodily Incarnation of the Logos in the man Jesus is seen as decisive also for the letters and symbols, which are used as vehicles of a higher insight? And in addition to that, it seems self-evident that the very fact that there is available for believers within the Church an interpretation of higher quality (such as Maximus himself represents through tradition) is due to the presence in the Christian community of Christ Himself through his Spirit. It is thus within the community of the Church, and its tradition of insight, that the deeper meaning of Scripture can be communicated.

"GNOSTIC" AND SACRAMENTAL COMMUNION

As a fourth question for closer consideration I mentioned the problem, to what extent there is a difference in Maximus's understanding between the "gnostic" communion with the Logos through Scripture and the sacramental communion with the Logos-Christ. It seems as if to Maximus the "gnostic" communion is only a part of the total possibility of communion. Since the *vita practica* for him is not just a stage to be passed (which it might have been to Evagrius), one might assert that sacramental communion with Christ means something that is relevant to the whole of man and his activity as a Christian. Thus, eucharistic communion should at least per-

[27]See *Cap. theol.* I, 89; *Patr. Gr.* 90, 1120 C.

[28]See *Cap. theol.* I, 90; *Patr. Gr.* 90, 1120 C; cf. *Amb.* 21; *Patr. Gr.* 91, 1244 D and 1253 CD.

[29]See *Cap. theol.* II, 14; *Patr. Gr.* 90, 1132 A.

tain to all the levels of man's composition. Further, there is also the aspect of experience (*peira*) to be underlined. Experience, however, is an ambiguous phenomenon in Maximus's understanding. It is only through the experience of Christ that the experience of Christian believers gets a decisive positive importance. Experience as true experience is one of pure presence beyond all sensible affection.[30] Thus, when experience is prepared by Christ and communicated by Him, it is essential to the quality of the Christian life.[31]

Therefore, the sacramental *peira* cannot be ruled out from the context of effective salvation. Besides, if "gnostic" participation and practical life are parallel, one can never exclude the possibility that even the most sensible experience of the sacraments may imply a connection with the more subtle dimension of spiritual progress. Maximus never, as we know, reduces the *vita practica* to being merely a preliminary stage, but keeps its importance at all stages of spiritual perfection. A special study could quite well be devoted to the function and role of experience in all the stages of the life of man (experience of blessedness before the fall, experience of the realities of fallen life as they present themselves to the senses, experience of Jesus Christ in regard to death and destruction, experience of the Christian through Christ of the new possibilities of life in Him, experiences of mystical union with God which intellectually and morally bring us back to revealed qualities of God in Law and Gospel, etc.).

ANALYSIS OF THE KEY TEXTS

In order to get further in our understanding of Maximus's view of the eucharist, however, we must now come to the detailed analysis of those texts in Maximus's work that refer explicitly to the eucharist in its aspect of real presence and communion.

[30]See *Quaest. ad Thal.* 60; *Patr. Gr.* 90, 625 A.

[31]On "experience" in Maximus, also see P. Miguel, "Peira. Contribution à l'étude du vocabulaire de l'expérience religieuse dans l'oeuvre de Maxime le Confesseur," *Studia Patristica* 7, 1966, pp. 355-361.

These texts are, to my understanding, not more than four. One of them is to be found in the *Quaestiones et Dubia* and the other three in the *Mystagogia*. (Other texts are only a supplement to this and cannot be properly interpreted in their possible eucharistic implication, unless one already has the key to their interpretation gained through an analysis of the four proper texts.)

Let us, then, start with *Qu. dub.* 41. It is against the background of the interpretation of the Holy Communion to be found in the Areopagite that this very short passage gets its interest. For here the question is why the number is unequal in the distribution of bread and wine. We remember that to Ps. Dionysius precisely the distribution as multiplication of something united into multiplicity was the symbolic (and also the sacramentally mysterious) point of the Holy Communion. But here, in Maximus, the interpretation goes in another direction. The unevenness of bread and chalice is said to point to the Divinity itself as being a single and non-composite Trinity.[32] Thus, to Maximus, the symbolic quality of the distribution of the gifts of the eucharist is not only "incarnational" as in Ps. Dionysius (where God distributes his gifts to "the many" of creation) but illuminative of God Himself, in that it points to the mystery of the Trinity (being one and three at the same time). This indicates that to Maximus the eucharist, and the Holy Communion particularly, is linked to the communion with the God-Three-in-One and not only, as in Ps. Dionysius, to the Divine One-ness, dividing itself communicatively to multiple creation thanks to the Incarnation. If to Ps. Dionysius the Communion refers to the descent (*katábasis*) of the Divinity only, to Maximus it also refers to the ascent (*anábasis*) in that it points to the Trinitarian mystery itself of One-ness-in-Multiplicity (ontologically united). It points to the fact that a certain multiplicity is of the divine essence.

The text we have now discussed may, of course, be isolated, but a closer analysis of the remaining texts (from the *Mystagogia*) seems to confirm the tendency. They too link the eucharistic communion with *deification*.

[32]See *Patr. Gr.* 90, 820 A.

A terminological study of these texts, together with the one just discussed, indicates certain very interesting coincidences. First of all, the discipline of silence, which Maximus feels obliged to, implies that Maximus takes his starting point at the liturgical moment immediately preceding communion (the later moments are there indicated by the words "and what follows"). Thus, we must not hesitate to look very carefully at what he says about the whole context, since it also pertains to "what follows." Secondly, the elements of communion are called "symbols" (*symbola*), and these *symbola* are directly related to what is communicated as *mysteria*.[33] In *Qu. Dub.* 41, the bread and the chalice are further called "representations" (*apeikonísmata*) of the divine essence.[34] In *Myst.* 21 and 24, the content of what is communicated is called *mysterion*, even "mysteries and archetypes."[35] Thus a *connection is established between the symbolical representations and the mysteries themselves.*

In *Myst.* 21, Maximus affirms that the communication (*metádosis*) of the mystery *"transforms"* into itself and demonstrates those who take part properly as becoming—by grace and participation—similar to its good Cause, and that thus nothing is missing in the divine presence with them.[36] We can see already here, then, that eucharistic communion is by Maximus related to the fulfillment of spiritual life and to man's deification. The terminology of eucharistic transformation (*metapoiesis*) is not used about the elements but about the believers. Thus, the demonstrative power of the eucharist, which to Ps. Dionysius was linked to the distribution, is in Maximus transferred to the receiving part and to the *reception* of the gifts. The presence (*parousía*) is further related to this effect: it is a presence that needs not be further fulfilled because it is demonstrated in the receivers in preparing them for their deification.

This is now further developed in the other texts of the *Mystagogia*. In Chapter 24, Maximus describes the com-

---

[33]In *Qu. Dub.* 41; *Patr. Gr.* 90, 820 A, the elements of the eucharist are called *symbola,* as is the case in *Myst.* 24; 91, 705 A.

[34]See *Patr. Gr.* 90, 820 A.

[35]See *ibid.,* 697 A, 704 D and 705 A.

[36]See *ibid.,* 697 A.

munion, the participation in the mysteries, as having the power to effect the fellowship (*koinonía*) and identity (*tautótes*) that are realized through the likeness (*homoiótes*), i.e. to God, a likeness through which man is made worthy to become God.[37] This is to say that Maximus here indicates that the eucharistic communion makes men, if they take part in it in a worthy way, into people who can receive the grace of deification, thanks to their established likeness to God. This is again something different from what we found in Ps. Dionysius. The sacrament has not only a demonstrative and appealing quality: *it is effective as the cause of that which is its final purpose, deification.* The effect is even further developed at the end of the same chapter, in that it is said there that Christ *transforms* us by conveying to us the *mysteries* contained in the sensible *symbols* and *archetypes* here present.[38] Thus we see that in the sacrament *Christ Himself is active* according to Maximus, again a motif absent in the interpretations of the Areopagite.

Finally, in the epilogue of the *Mystagogia*, Maximus again refers to the communion. He affirms that it demonstrates the application of our "sonship" with God (already established through baptism, as we know from Maximus's more explicit interpretations of that sacrament) and our union, affinity, and likeness (*homoiótes*), and deification (*theôsis*), through which God may be one in all.[39] Thus, we see that Maximus, through his careful and humble indications in the margin of his elucidations of other moments of the liturgy in proximity to the act of communion, is able to develop a true theology of eucharistic communion definitely linked to deification (the ultimate stage of Christian development, entirely dependent on divine grace). In its approach it is surprisingly different from that of the Areopagite, although it is to him that he refers throughout his *Mystagogia*.

37*Ibid.,* 704 D.
38*Ibid.*; 705 A.
39*Ibid.*; 709 C.

THE QUESTION OF THE "WORTHY" RECEIVER

Thus, we have only one of the questions left out of those that were indicated before: to what extent in Maximus's understanding of eucharistic communion is *the principle of analogy* implied, so that what is given is measured after the capacity of the receiver to receive? My presupposition is that according to a "realistic" understanding of the eucharist a distinction must be made between an objective and a subjective factor, i.e. between the objective presence of the fullness of Christ in the eucharistic elements and the subjectively determined mode of reception of the receiver. For a "symbolistic" understanding this problem presents itself otherwise. From the texts of Maximus we have analyzed it seems clear that the principle of analogy is involved.

Now, the formula of that principle in Maximus is the famous *tantum-quantum* formula, which found its most expressive representation in *Amb.* 10. There it is clearly based on the distinctive presupposition of Maximus that God and man are exemplars (*paradeigmata*) of one another. This means that the deification of man is dependent on the Incarnation of the Logos, but also that the degree of enfleshment *in* man is decisive for the degree of deification *of* man.[40] What Maximus speaks about in the *Mystagogia* is a decisive likeness (*homoiótes*), but the character of this likeness is not quite clear. Is it a "katabatic" likeness to us, inherent in the bodily form of the sacrament, or is it a produced likeness in man which makes him receptive to the divine gifts of the sacrament? In *Myst.* 21, Maximus clearly talks about a divine "sharing" that transforms the receivers into itself (i.e. to likeness unto itself) and through grace and participation shows those who worthily take part as similar (*hómoioi*) to the Good Cause. But the character of that worthiness is not precisely defined. In *Myst.* 24, it is said that community and identity are received *through likeness* without further clarification of where this likeness lies.

[40]*Patr. Gr.* 91, 1113 BC.

But in the epilogue of the *Mystagogia* the central text says
that the participation (i.e. communion) makes clear our
sonship, union, and affinity as well as our divine likeness and
deification because of the goodness of God. In a passage of
Myst. 23, likewise, the forthcoming communion seems to be
referred to as the reception by grace into sonship through
similarity.[41] Thus I feel entitled to conclude that the *likeness*
which is referred to here is in the first place that of the sacrament to the divine reality, and secondarily that of the receiver
in relation to what is received, thanks to his degree of receptiveness. If that is correct, what Maximus wants to say is
that *the incarnational likeness of the sacrament receives the
responsive likeness of the communicant into itself and transforms it into the likeness of human deification.*

The famous distinction of the Areopagite in the *Coel.
Hierarchia* II between similar and dissimilar symbols[42] might
have had an influence on Maximus at this point. But then
the difference between certain scriptural symbols and those
of the sacrament must be such that if dissimilar symbols in
the Scripture can be more helpful, since they remind us of the
incomprehensibility of God, nevertheless (and that is Maximus's own evaluation) the incarnational similarity of the
symbols of eucharistic presence and communion are effective
in establishing that similarity of man with God, which is the
realization of his character as *imago Dei.* Thus, *through
communion man,* who worthily demonstrates by virtuous
preparation his receptiveness, *is brought by grace through the
sacrament into that sphere of human spiritual development
where deification is realized.*

If my contention is correct, Maximus wants to say that
eucharistic communion, through being in the perfect likeness
with the Logos made man, effects in man, properly prepared,
the likeness of man with God that goes beyond his natural
qualities and deifies him according to the *tantum-quantum*
principle. But here, also, the perspective of Maximus is other
than that of the Areopagite. If the latter is primarily interested in the reflecting quality of symbols, Maximus insists on

[41]*Patr. Gr.* 91, 701 B.
[42]See *Patr. Gr.* 3, 140 C-141 A.

an *incarnational* perspective, where the elevation of man is the direct fruit of the descent of the Logos, of his "becoming thick," in successive stages of the economy of divine salvation. Maximus deals in his *Mystagogia,* first of all, with the effect of the eucharistic communion, i.e. with the subjective and receiving side of it (possibly on account of his position as a layman). He presupposes also an objective and effective side of Christ's own action (of established similarity with the divine/human reality of the incarnate Logos) as the necessary cause of the fruits of communion. It is in regard to that side that he keeps the "discipline of silence." Maximus thus definitely indicates a proper theology of the eucharist, and it does not at all necessarily coincide with that of the Areopagite, although he depends on the latter's way of presentation.

This is clearly in accord with his own incarnational vision, where the movements of descent and ascent are in a constant dialectical relationship. The Origenist monism and a Dionysian modified Neoplatonism are radically transcended.

It remains to be demonstrated what his other authority on the matter, the mysterious "Old Man" (probably Sophronius), in fact contributed to this eucharistic theology.

Bibliography

The complete works in Greek are to be found in J. P. Migne, *Patrologia Graeca*, vols. 90-91, Paris 1865.

Quaestiones ad Thalassium I–LV are edited in C. Laga-C. Steel, *Maximi Confessoris Quaestiones ad Thalassium I, Quaestiones I–LV, una cum latina interpretatione Ioannis Scottae Eriugenae iuxta posita*, Leuven University Press, Turnhout-Brepols, 1980.

Translations into English:

St. Maximus the Confessor, *The Ascetic Life. The Four Centuries on Charity*. Translated and Annotated by Polycarp Sherwood, O.S.B., S.T.D. The Newman Press, Westminster, Maryland and Longmans, Green and Co., London, 1955.

Translations into French:

Saint Maxime le Confesseur, *Le Mystère du Salut*. Textes traduits et présentés par Astérios Argyriou. Avec une introduction de I.-H. Dalmais, O.P., Les Éditions du Soleil levant, Namur 1964.

Maxime le Confesseur, *Lettre à Jean le Cubiculaire sur la charité*, in *La Vie Spirituelle* 79 (1948), pp. 296-303.

Maxime le Confesseur, *Centuries sur la Charité*. Introduction et traduction de Joseph Pegon, S.J., Éditions du Cerf, Paris–Édition de l'Abeille, Lyon, 1943.

Saint Maxime, moine et confesseur, Brève interprétation de la Prière de Notre Père (Mt 6/9-13) pour un ami du Christ in Alain Riou, *Le monde et l'église selon Maxime le Confesseur*, Beauchesne, Paris 1973, pp. 214-239 and *Cent chapitres sur la théologie et l'économie dans la chair du Fils de Dieu I, ibid.*, pp. 240-261.

Maxime le Confesseur, *Trois grands textes de Maxime sur l'agonie écrits entre 642 et 646* in François-Marie Léthel, *Théologie de l'agonie du Christ. La liberté humaine du Fils*

175

de Dieu et son importance sotériologique mises en lumiere par saint Maxime le Confesseur, Editions Beauchesne, Paris 1979, pp. 123-126.

Translations into German:

Maximus der Bekenner, *All-eins in Christus.* Auswahl, Übertragung, Einleitung von Endre von Ivanka, Johannes Verlag, Einsiedeln 1961.

Maximus der Bekenner, *Die Mystagogie* in Hans Urs von Balthasar, *Kosmische Liturgie. Das Weltbild Maximus des Bekenners,* Johannes-Verlag, Einsiedeln, 1961, pp. 366-407, *Viermal hundert Sprüche über die Liebe, ibid., pp.* 408-481 and *Die gnostischen Centurien* (with comments) in *ibid.,* pp. 482-643.

LITERATURE

Hans Urs von Balthasar, *Kosmische Liturgie. Das Weltbild Maximus des Bekenners,* Zweite, völlig veränderte Auflage. Johannes-Verlag, Einsiedeln 1961.

René Bornert, *Les Commentaires Byzantins de la Divine Liturgie du VIIe au XVe siècle,* Paris 1966.

_____ "Explication de la liturgie et interprétation de l'écriture chez Maxime le Confesseur," in *Studia Patristica* 10, Akademie Verlag, Berlin 1976, pp. 323-327.

P. Canart, "La deuxiéme lettre à Thomas de S. Maxime le Confesseur," in *Byzantion* 34 (1964), pp. 415-449.

Irénée-Henri Dalmais, O.P., "S. Maxime le Confesseur. Docteur de la Charité," in *La Vie Spirituelle* 1948, pp. 296-303.

_____ "La théorie des 'Logoi' des créatures chez s. Maxime le Confesseur," in *Revue des Sciences Philosophiques et Théologiques* 36 (1952), pp. 244-249.

_____ "L'oeuvre spirituelle de s. Maxime le Confesseur," in *La Vie Spirituelle. Suppl.* 21 (1952), pp. 216-226.

_____ "La doctrine ascétique de s. Maxime le Confesseur d'après le Liber asceticus," in *Irénikon* 26 (1953), pp. 17-39.

_____ "Un traité de théologie contemplative: Le commentaire du Pater Noster de s. Maxime le Confesseur," in *Revue d' Ascétique et de Mystique* 29 (1953), pp. 123-159.

_____ "L'anthropologie spirituelle de saint Maxime le Confesseur," in *Recherches et Débats* 36 (1961), pp. 202-211.

_____ "La fonction unificatrice du Verbe Incarné dans les oeuvres spirituelles de saint Maxime le Confesseur," in *Sciences Ecclésiastiques* 14 (1962), pp. 449-459.

_____ "L'héritage évagrien dans la synthèse de saint Maxime le Confesseur," in *Studia Patristica* 8 (1966), pp. 356-362.

_____ "Mystère liturgique et divinisation dans la Mystagogie de saint Maxime le Confesseur," in *Epektasis. Mélanges patristiques offerts au Cardinal Jean Daniélou,* Paris 1972, pp. 55-62.

Jean Daniélou S.J., *Philon d'Alexandrie,* Librairie Arthème Fayard, Paris 1958.

Juan Miguel Garrigues, O.P., *Maxime le Confesseur. La charité, avenir divin de l'homme,* Éditions Beauchesne, Paris 1976.

Irénée Hausherr, S.J., *Philautie. De la tendresse pour soi à la charité selon saint Maxime le Confesseur.* (Orientalia Christiana Analecta 137). Pont. Institutum Orientalium Studiorum, Rome 1952.

Felix Heinzer, *Gottes Sohn als Mensch. Die Struktur des Menschseins Christi bei Maximus Confessor,* Universitätsverlag, Freiburg, Switzerland 1980.

Felix Heinzer and Christoph von Schönborn (ed.), *Maximus Confessor. Actes du Symposium sur Maxime le Confesseur, Fribourg, 2-5 septembre 1980,* Éditions Universitaires, Fribourg, Switzerland 1982.

François-Marie Léthel, *Théologie de l'agonie du Christ. La liberté humaine du Fils de Dieu et son importance sotériologique mises en lumière par saint Maxime le Confesseur,* Éditions Beauchesne, Paris 1979.

Vladimir Lossky, *The Mystical Theology of the Eastern Church,* James Clarke & Co. Ltd., London 1957.

John Meyendorff, *Byzantine Theology. Historical Trends and Doctrinal Themes,* Fordham University Press, Bronx, N.Y., 1974.

_____ *St. Gregory Palamas and Orthodox Spirituality,* St. Vladimir's Seminary Press, New York 1974.

P. Miguel, "Peira. Contribution à l'étude du vocabulaire de l'expérience religieuse dans l'oeuvre de Maxime le Confesseur," in *Studia Patristica* 7, Akademie Verlag, Berlin 1966, pp. 355-361.

Jaroslav Pelikan, *The Christian Tradition. A History of the Development of Doctrine, 2: The Spirit of Eastern Christendom (600-1700),* The University of Chicago Press, Chicago 1974.

Christoph von Schönborn, O.P., *Sophrone de Jérusalem. Vie monas-tique et confession dogmatique,* Editions universitaries, Fribourg, Switzerland 1976.

Alain Riou, O.P., *Le monde et l'église selon Maxime le Confesseur,* Éditions Beauchesne, Paris 1972.

_____ *L'Icone du Christ. Fondements théologiques élaborés entre le Ier et le IIe Concile de Nicée (325-787),* Éditions Universitaires, Fribourg, Switzerland 1976.

Polycarp Sherwood, O.S.B., *Date-List of the Works of Maximus the Confessor.* Studia Anselmiana 30, Herder, Rome 1952.

_____ *The Earlier Ambigua of St. Maximus the Confessor.* Studia Anselmiana 36, Herder, Rome 1955.

_____ *St. Maximus the Confessor: The Ascetic Life. Centuries on Charity.* Translated and Annotated. Ancient Christian Writers 21, The Newman Press, Westminster, Maryland 1955.

_____ "Survey of Recent Work on St. Maximus the Confessor," in *Traditio* 20 (1964), pp. 428-437.

René Roques, *L'univers Dionysien. Structure hiérarchique du monde selon le Pseudo-Denys,* Aubier, Paris 1954.

Théologie de la vie monastique, Aubier, Paris 1961.

Lars Thunberg, *Microcosm and Mediator. The Theological Anthro-pology of Maximus the Confessor.* (Acta Seminarii Neotesta-mentici Upsaliensis XXV.) C.W.K. Gleerup, Lund and Einar Munksgaard, Copenhagen 1965.

Walther Völker, *Kontemplation und Ekstase bei Pseudo-Dionysius Areopagita,* Franz Steiner Verlag, Wiesbaden 1958.

_____ *Maximus Confessor als Meister des geistlichen Lebens,* Franz Steiner Verlag, Wiesbaden 1965.

Index